YVONNE
COLORS CHANGING HUE
PORCELLA

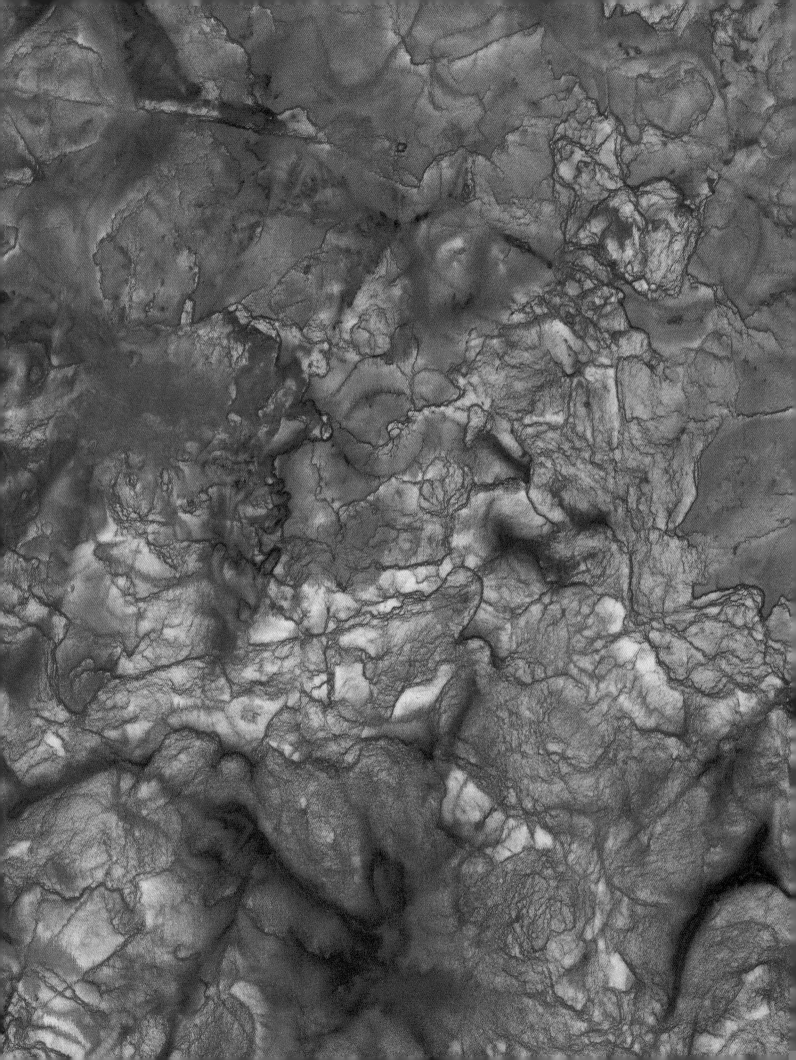

YVONNE PORCELLA
COLORS CHANGING HUE

To Dixie

Experiment & Enjoy Colors

Yvonne Porcella
Feb. 9, 1995

C&T PUBLISHING

Graphic illustrations by Jill K. Maxwell Berry, Artista Artworks

Edited by Harold Nadel

Technical information edited by Joyce Engels Lytle

Book design by Jill K. Maxwell Berry, Artista Artworks, San Diego

Photography by Sharon Risedorph, San Francisco
Author photograph by Elaine Faris Keenan, Mill Valley

Library of Congress Cataloging-in-Publication Data
Porcella, Yvonne
    Colors changing hue / Yvonne Porcella
       p.   cm.
    ISBN 0-914881-86-8
    1. Textile painting.   2. Textile crafts.   I. Title.
    TT851.P67 1994
    746.6--dc20   94-13305

Bernina is a registered trademark of Fritz Gegauf, Ltd.
Cloud Cover and Lumière are trademarks of Cerulean Blue Ltd.
Cotton Classic, Low Loft, and Poly-fil are registered trademarks of Fairfield Processing Corporation.
Createx is a trademark of Color Craft, Ltd.
Deka Permanent Fabric Paint is a registered trademark of Decart, Inc.
FabriColor and FabricMate are products of Yasutomo & Company.
Interference and Liquitex are registered trademarks of Binney & Smith.
Jacquard is a registered trademark of Rupert, Gibbon & Spider, Inc.
Kreinik Cord and Ombré are brand names of Kreinik Mfg. Co., Inc.
Niji is a brand name of Yasutomo & Company.
Omnigrid is a registered trademark of Omnigrid Inc.
Pearlescent Liquid Acrylic is a brand name of Daler-Rowney.
Pilot is a registered trademark of the Pilot Pen Corporation of America.
Setacolor is a registered trademark of Pebeo France.
Thermore is a registered trademark of Hobbs Bonded Fibers.
Tulip is a registered trademark of Polymerics, Inc.
UHU stic and Uni are registered trademarks of FaberCastell Corporation.
Versatex is a brand name of Siphon Art.
Wonder-Under is a trademark of Freudenberg Nonwovens, Pellon Division.

Published by C&T Publishing
P. O. Box 1456
Lafayette, California 94549

Printed in Hong Kong
10 9 8 7 6 5 4 3 2 1

Table of Contents

Introduction 9

Chapter 1
Equipment & Materials
Equipment 11
Fabric Paints 12
Fabrics 13
Ribbons and Roses 14

Chapter 2
Paint Techniques
Applying Paint to Fabric 17
Using Up Excess Paint 19
Overpainting..............................19
Spray Painting............................19
Sun Painting...............................20
Sponge Painting..........................20
Heat Set the Colors......................20
Painting Ribbon..........................21
Clean Up 21

Chapter 3
Sewing & Embellishment
Working with Cotton.....................23
Working with Silk........................23
Thread 23
Strip Piecing Silk........................23
Folded Fabric Overlay 25
Silk Ribbon Embellishments...........25
Hand Appliqué 25
Burned Silk Appliqué 26
Foundation Fabric 27
Tools for Trimming.......................27
Seam Allowance 27
Seam Binding.............................27
Quilt Sleeve 27

Chapter 4
Quilts, Blocks, & Wall Hangings
Burned Silk Appliqué Grapes 29
Strip Piecing, Log Cabin Style 30
Cotton Appliqué Wall Hanging 31
Rose And Green Silk Small Quilt 34
Summer Bouquet Silk Quilt 36

Chapter 5
Vests
Vest with Armhole Band....................45
General Directions for
    Vest Construction 46
Strip Pieced Vest with Armhole
    Band 48
Wisteria Vest with Burned
    Silk Appliqué 51
Pleated Surface Vest with Appliqué ...54
Gold Vest With Appliqué 59

Chapter 6
Cloth Dolls
General Directions For Dolls.............65
Brenda 68
Honey 71
Sweetie......................................73
Lilac Lyla 75
Lyla-san 79

Chapter 7
Gifts & Wrapping
Collage Heart 83
Harvest Heart..........................85
Stuffed Heart..........................87
Wrapping 89
Bags......................................91
Ribbons 91

Resource Guide..............................94

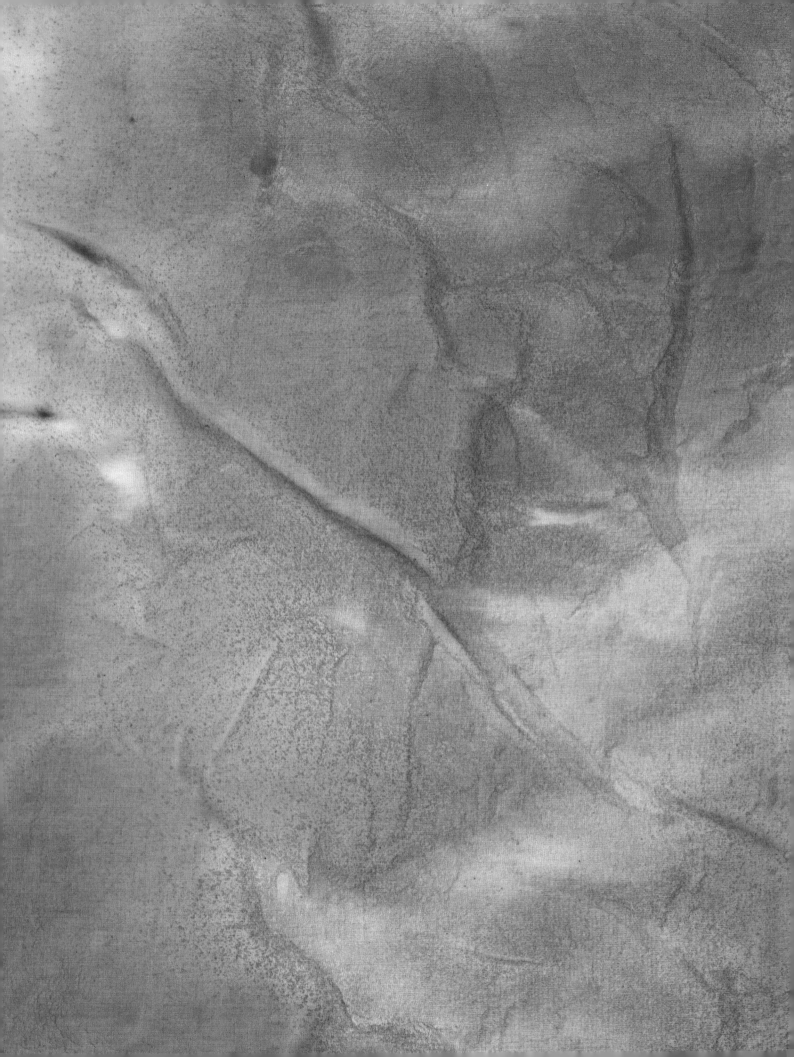

Acknowledgments

Those who are familiar with my career know that my educational training was in the sciences, including a degree in nursing. After 18 years in that occupation, I launched a new life in art, teaching, and publishing. I often think back to my first year in college, to the English teacher who pointed to me and announced to the class that I would never graduate because I had no imagination. Fortunately, I interpreted his revelation not as a defeat but as a challenge. All that I do as author and artist is the result of learning from life's experiences and using that learning creatively. I have used my natural sense for color imaginatively, and I am grateful for the gift.

This is my sixth adventure in the world of authorship and publishing. It seems a lifetime ago when, in 1977, I decided to print a small black-and-white book, *Five Ethnic Patterns*. This consisted of garment patterns suitable for weavers, quilters, and stitchers. Although I had no prior experience, I quickly learned to do graphics, typesetting, layout, advertising, distribution, inventory control, etc. I made some mistakes but, on the whole, my experiences as author and publisher were successful. As I wrote and published more books, each became bigger and more colorful, and I learned more each time. The culmination of many years of making wearable art and quilts came in 1986, when I published *A Colorful Book*. For this, I drew upon the expertise of two very special people, Roderick Kiracofe as producer and designer and Harold Nadel as editor. Both are very important to me, and I am proud to call them friends.

When I was finally ready to create another book, it was Harold Nadel who came to my aid and suggested that I submit the proposal to C&T Publishing. I am grateful to Todd Hensley and to the extraordinary people who are C&T Publishing for allowing me to share this new book with you, and for reprinting and distributing three of my previous books.

Every book requires the unseen support of special people in the life of the author. Janice Rhea and Kay Elson have been trusted friends throughout my endeavors, and they wisely get my early manuscripts on track. I am immensely grateful to Maggie Brosnan, Steve Kalar, and Holley Junker, artists all and special confidants. Thanks to Joyce Lytle, who did a wonderful job with technical editing for this book, to Sharon Risedorph for flawless photography, and to Jill K. Maxwell Berry for beautiful book design. The Wandering Irishman gives me strength and encouragement, and I am eternally grateful for his confidence in my talents.

My husband, Bob, has been my greatest asset: he helps me to be who I am. I appreciate the unconditional love of our wonderful children Steve, Suzanne, Greg, and Don, daughters-in-law Sandy and Madhu, son-in-law Tim, and grandchildren Nick, Vince, Eric, Mikey, Mimi, Tori, Sarina, and Elizabeth.

To all the other special people in my life, I extend thanks for your friendship, encouragement, and patience.

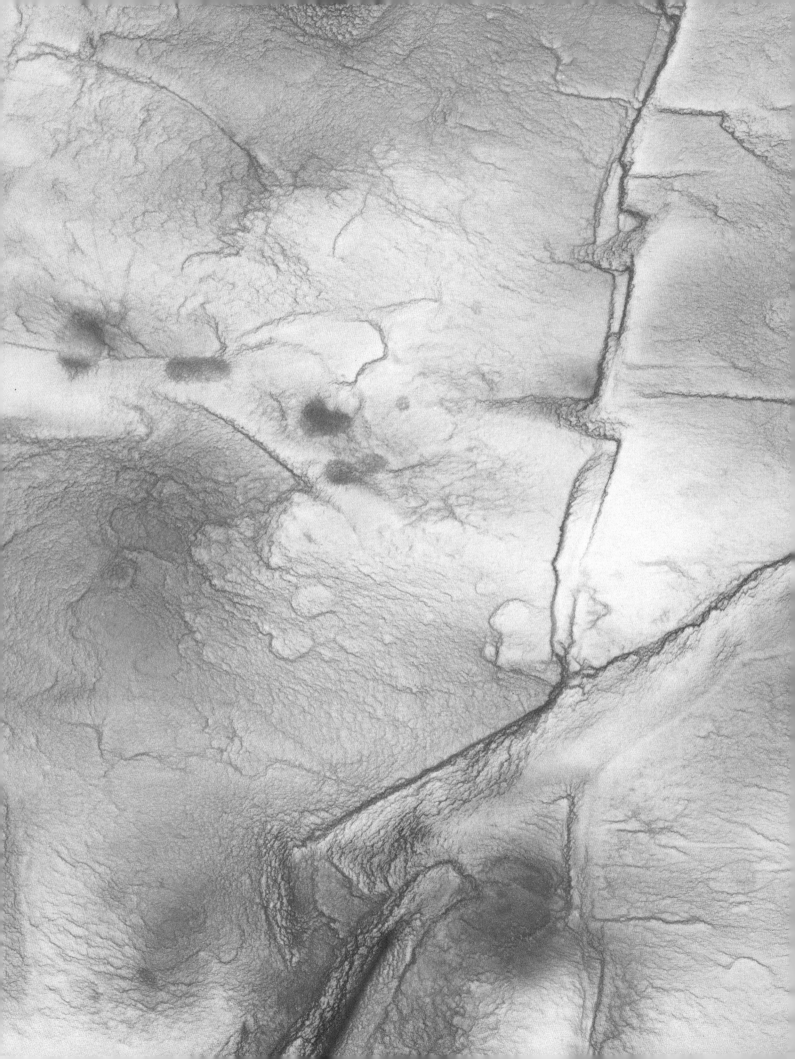

Introduction

With so many beautiful print fabrics in the stores, why would you consider creating your own fabric? When you have made the fabric, how would you use it? In this book I present a very basic method for fabric painting and a variety of projects to make with the fabric, including quilts, vests, dolls, and gifts. I encourage you to make your own painted fabric. However, you can make these projects with fabrics that you buy from your local store or at a quilt show. There are artists who sell painted or dyed fabric, and companies produce fabrics that look hand-colored.

Fabric painting is exciting because it offers you a personal choice of color and fabric. Painted fabric gives a distinctive look to projects. Although fabric painting is easy, it is often misunderstood. People believe they have to know how to draw in order to know how to paint, or think they should take art classes and buy lots of expensive equipment. Because I have developed a personal approach to fabric painting and I have taught many classes, I can offer a very easy and successful process. Mixing color, a major stumbling block to most people, is simple to learn using these methods. My goal is to allow the paint to react with the fabric so that the color pattern is abstract. There are no specific skills required, except to let the paint dry on the fabric! How you apply the paint is the key to success. There are no complicated color wheels, formulas for mixing paint, or time-consuming methods for color fixing. Around your home is the equipment you need to begin. The fabric and painting supplies are readily available by mail order. You may have to visit your local hardware store for a few items, and expect to buy a few artist brushes.

The fabric paint I use is acrylic and formulated specifically for natural-fiber fabrics. It is water-soluble and made permanent by heat-setting with an iron. The transparent colors can be thinned with water, creating a beautiful watercolor effect. There are many products on the market: I will tell you which are my favorites and what you can substitute. Suppliers are listed in the resource guide in the back of the book.

So, let's begin.

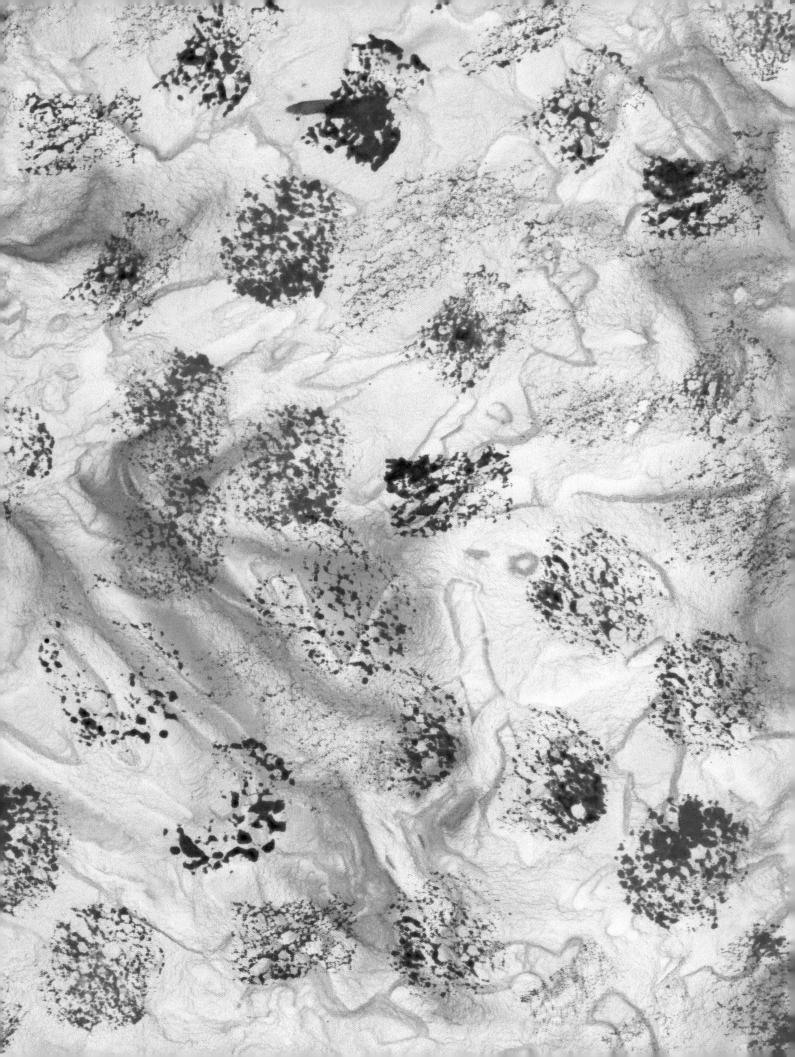

Equipment & Materials

You can buy fabric paint and fabric by mail order. Almost all the basic equipment can be found around the home.

Equipment

Equipment Around the Home

- Assorted glass or plastic containers: margarine tubs, wide-mouth jars, etc.
- Large basin: dishwashing tub, or any basin about 6" deep
- Two disposable aluminum pie pans
- Quart jar for clean water
- Quart jar for washing brushes
- Dishwashing soap for brushes and clean-up
- Spray bottle for water
- Old towel for clean-up
- Two kitchen sponges, 2¾" x 4½" x ½", one for clean-up and one to cut into shapes
- Tongue depressors or popsicle sticks
- Paper towels
- Sink or a large bucket of water
- Old clothes or an apron
- Rubber gloves are necessary only if you have manicured nails. The acrylic paint will stain nail polish.

Equipment from the Hardware Store

- Clear plastic 9' x 12' dropcloth, 0.9 to 1.5 mil. thickness
- 1" wide brush

Equipment from Art Supply Store

- Two artist's acrylic brushes: round bristle #8
- Liquitex® Acrylic artist color: 2 fl. oz. tube of iridescent gold

Additional Paint Supplies for Advanced Projects

- Gold and silver marking pens, extra-fine and medium points: Pilot®, Niji™, or Uni®
- Liquitex Interference®, 2 fl. oz. jar
- Pearlescent™ liquid acrylic inks, l fl. oz. jar
- Metallic fabric paints: gold and pearl white
- Permanent fabric pens: FabriColor™ or FabricMate™ green, pink, and lavender
- Artist's brush, #6 flat tapered end

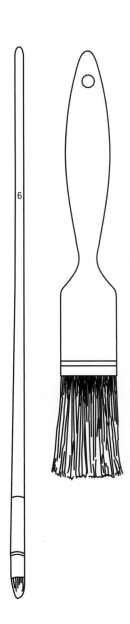

Above (Pictured smaller than actual size): Artist's acrylic round brush #8

For advanced projects: #6 flat tapered-end acrylic brush

Brush from hardware store, 1" wide

Fabric Paints

You can buy fabric paints at some art and craft stores and by mail order. Be sure to purchase *transparent fabric paint* and not fabric dye. Dye is a chemical which requires complex methods of application and setting. Dye is sometimes called silk paint or silk dye.

Fabric paints I have tested are Setacolor® Transparent (my preference), Jacquard®, Versatex®, and Createx™ Textile Colors. Most fabric paints are compatible and can be used with other brands, such as Jacquard with Setacolor. The fabric paints which are metallic, and Liquitex iridescent paint, will also mix with any of the other brands.

I have not tested other paints available, such as Deka® Permanent Fabric Paint, Cloud Cover™, and Lumière™.

Paint Colors (see photos on pages 19 and 20)

You are tempted by many available colors. I prefer to limit the colors I buy and change the basic hue. My method for fabric painting is to use only one color, with the addition of black or iridescent paint to alter the original hue slightly. The beginner can start with primary red, blue, and yellow, plus black—for example Setacolor cardinal red, cobalt blue, buttercup, and black lake, in 45 ml. (1.5 oz) bottles. Cardinal red with black makes mauve. Cobalt blue with black makes indigo. Buttercup with black makes gold. (See Applying Paint to Fabric on page 17.)

After experimenting with these basic colors, you can try mixing two primary colors together. Yellow with a small amount of blue produces green; add more yellow to make yellow-green. Red mixed with blue produces purple. Yellow with red makes orange. After mixing these colors, add a few drops of black so these colors will be most compatible with the other mixed colors you have already made. If you would like a reference for colors, the simplest tool is a color wheel. This is usually available at art supply or paint stores. I have found that the best method is trial mixing: you will learn by practice.

After experimenting with the primary and secondary colors, you can increase the range of color possibilities by buying additional colors: ultramarine, Bengal pink, emerald, velvet brown, Parma violet, sienna, turquoise.

Suggested Color Mixtures

I have experimented with Setacolor, but I do not keep a precise record of each color. I just mix the colors until I find one that I like. The following list is what I mixed to paint the fabrics used in this book: they can be made from the basic hue, adding small amounts of the additional color until you reach the desired shade.

Ultramarine with black makes midnight blue. Bengal pink with black makes a dusty rose; add more black to make burgundy. Emerald with black deepens the green to a dark forest green; dilute the mixture and add a small amount of blue to make moss green. Velvet brown can be mixed with buttercup and black to make an old gold. Adding Liquitex gold to this mixture will make an iridescent gold. Sienna can be mixed with black to make brick. Turquoise with black is darker than indigo. To make peach, use buttercup with Bengal pink to make orange and then add black or ultramarine. Periwinkle is made by mixing cobalt blue with Parma violet. Dilute velvet brown will make tan; add a small amount of cardinal red to make taupe. Cardinal red with velvet brown and black makes rust. Cardinal red with iridescent gold makes rosebud. Orange with red and a touch of black makes pomegranate. Iridescent gold or pearlized white can be added to any paint mixture to add sparkle.

Gray

To make your own gray, dilute 2 tablespoons black in one pint of water. Add a primary color to the gray to change the gray slightly (yellow will brighten the gray, blue will cool it, red will warm it). Gray can also be made by mixing equal parts of orange and blue.

Multicolors

A multicolored fabric can be made with any combination; each color should be applied and allowed to sit for a minute on the fabric before you add another color. Some interesting colors result from the mixture on the wet fabric. Do not be concerned if the fabric colors are not what you expect: the fabric is always usable as a backing of a quilt, or it can be cut into small pieces to use in projects.

Fabrics

The fabrics to use are natural fiber, such as 100% cotton or silk. Most of the paint manufacturers list which fabrics are compatible with their products. My usual preference for projects is 100% cotton muslin, glazed white cotton chintz, or a variety of silk fabrics. The projects in this book should be made with either 100% cotton or silk. I have had success using Setacolor and Versatex on a blend of 65% cotton to 35% polyester, but test the fabrics first to be sure the paint is color-fast and light-fast on the fabric blends.

Different pure white cottons and silks suitable for painting are available by mail order; suppliers are listed in the Resource Guide in the back of the book. Some of the cottons made specifically for painting do not have sizing and can be expensive. For the beginner I recommend using 100% cotton muslin, available as quilter's muslin. If this fabric is labeled as permanent press, I wash it first in hot water to remove the finish. If the muslin is unbleached, the painted fabric will have a slightly different color than if the muslin is bleached. I use unbleached muslin and personally like the different texture it offers. This book features transparent paint techniques to use on white fabrics. Colored fabrics require opaque textile paints.

Silk

Silk fabrics present a new challenge. Sewing with silk is very rewarding: the results are beautiful, but some experimentation is needed. White silk fabrics suitable for painting are very inexpensive, especially if you buy a large quantity from a mail-order supplier. I like to have enough fabric for experimentation, and it is much easier to be free to try new colors when the fabric is at hand. If you use one or two yards of costly fabric, you will avoid taking risks, and you will not learn as much or have as many unplanned successes. Some of my most beautiful fabrics resulted from bits of leftover paints. Rather than waste the paint or pour it down the drain, I use it on extra fabric. Many of the projects in this book require small amounts of a variety of colors, and these bonus fabrics afford you a large available color selection.

Silks offer a great variety of weaves and styles; you should know a few facts about silk before you buy. Mail-order catalogues describe the fabrics and offer fabric samples for a small fee. The silk is priced by the yard or meter, and it is listed by type and weight. Type of silk refers to the name and weave. Silk weight refers to the mummy weight, sometimes listed as mommie, mummie, or mm. The larger the mummy number, the heavier the silk. Silk Habotai 5mm is an evenly woven, very lightweight silk. Silk Dupion 19mm is a textured heavyweight silk. Some silks do not list a mm weight because the weight is standard for the type of silk. Each silk project in this book will list the type I have used: Silk Twill 10 mm, Phoenix Pongee, Charmeuse Silk Satin plain-back, Silk Organza sheer, or Spun Silk, which I purchase by mail order. Suppliers suggest that silk be wet before painting, to insure the removal of residual silk gum. Pongee is one type of silk that has a stiffness caused by the gum in the fabric. Sometimes this residual can give wonderful variations in color; ignore the rule to pre-wet the fabric. On page 17, when I explain applying paint to fabric, I discuss wet versus dry fabric and the different applications.

Ribbons and Roses

Many of the book projects use narrow silk ribbon as embellishment. It is offered in three widths; for these projects I used 3.8 mm (sometimes listed as 3.5 mm or 4 mm). There are many color choices, but I prefer to buy white and paint it to match the projects.

Wider silk ribbon can be formed into small roses. Different styles of ribbon roses are available by mail order in a variety of colors featuring buds, full roses, and clusters with green leaves. Elsie's Exquisiques offers a good selection of silk ribbons and ribbon roses; the address is listed in the Resource Guide. Craft stores also sell small packets of synthetic ribbon roses. Although they are stiffer than silk roses, they can be substituted and the white ones can be painted.

Wire-edged ribbons have become very popular in quilt projects. The ribbon is available in many colors, and white ribbon can be painted. This ribbon is not silk, but it is compatible with all the projects in this book. I cannot guarantee that all wire-edged ribbons are colorfast; you should test a small sample if you intend to wash your finished project. If you are sewing the ribbon down on the surface of a vest or a quilt, the ends of the ribbon should be tapered and the wires pulled out and clipped back to at least ½" from the ends.

Chapter Two

Paint Techniques

Applying Paint to Fabric

Assemble all the tools, cotton or silk, and paints. Begin by preparing the work surface. Be aware that some home surfaces are vulnerable to fabric paint. It can permanently stain concrete, unfinished wood, rugs, walls, and clothes if accidentally spilled. Protect exposed surfaces with plastic or newspaper, and wear old clothes. Even if a spill is caught immediately, depending on the type of material and the intensity of the color, the paint may not come out. *Be cautious!*

Unfold the plastic dropcloth a few days before painting and wrinkle it up to eliminate the regular folds. These folds form subtle hills and valleys, and wet fabric painted on top of the plastic could dry and retain the image of the folds. Cut the dropcloth into small pieces to accommodate the size of the fabric and table, and spread the dropcloth over the work table. Have water available in the spray bottle, as well as one quart jar of clean water and one quart jar of water to wash brushes. In a plastic tub or glass jar, pour about ¼ cup of water. Since I experiment and do not measure the water or the paint, these measurements are suggestions. Pour a small amount of your chosen color of paint, about two teaspoons, into the water and dip a tongue depressor or popsicle stick into the black; add a few drops of black to the mixture. Stir to mix. With the acrylic bristle round #8 brush, test the color on a small piece of fabric. The color will dry slightly lighter. Thin the color with more water for a lighter value, or add more primary hue to darken. Be careful with the black: add only small amounts at a time, then test the color.

Painting on a Flat Surface

Begin with half a yard of fabric to see how the technique works, and use larger pieces after experimenting. Wet the fabric with cold water in the sink or large bucket, and wring out the excess. The wrinkles that develop in the fabric will help to enhance the painted pattern. Spread the wet fabric over the dropcloth. The wet fabric will dilute the color mixture to make a watercolor pastel. For a darker fabric, add more fabric paint to the paint mixture. Use the 1" brush or the artist's round brush to apply the paint to the fabric. Dip the brush into the paint mixture and touch the fabric with the brush in a random pattern. Let the color flow into the fabric. The paint will drift across the surface, so allow time for this reaction. Add more paint to the unpainted areas until the whole piece is colored. Let the fabric dry on the plastic. When the fabric has dried, subtle patterns of color develop to form an interesting pattern. (Read the Caution on page 20.)

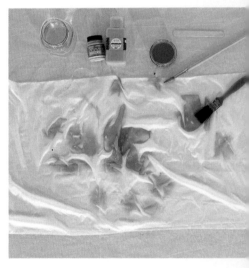

Painting on a flat surface

Painting in a Pan or Basin

With the remaining paint, experiment with another painting technique. Again wet the fabric and wring out excess water. Place the fabric in the pie pan. Crumple up the fabric so it fits into the pan. The pan will hold one yard of 10mm silk. For cotton fabric, use a larger basin. Apply the paint with the 1" brush to the top surface of the fabric. Press the paint from the brush into the fabric. Let the fabric sit for a few minutes, then turn the fabric and apply more paint. Continue applying paint until all the white areas are covered. Let the fabric dry in the pan. Turn the fabric over to rearrange it in the pan after 2 hours. This technique will give a very different effect from the earlier one. The fabric confined to this small pan will form hills and valleys and, when the paint dries, it will be very dark in certain areas. Stop this process by removing the fabric from the pan and laying the fabric flat to dry. This technique works well when black has been added to the primary color.

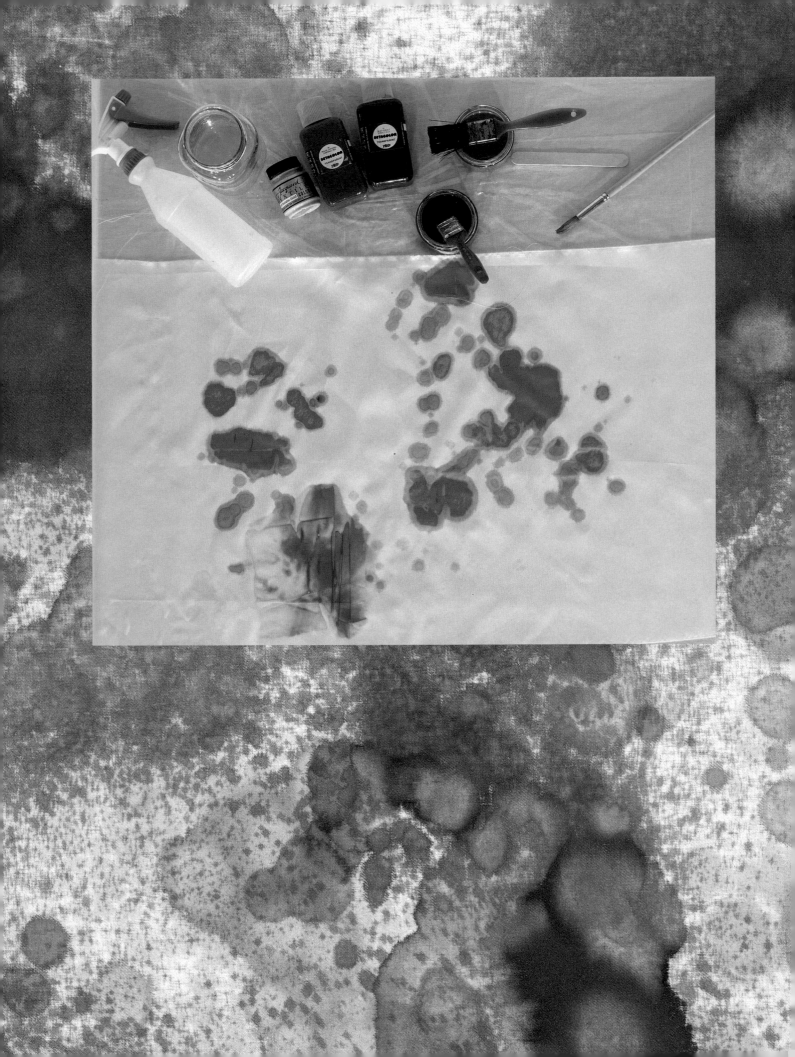

Painting Dry Fabric

Another technique is to apply the paint mixture to a dry piece of fabric, creating a slightly darker color. Be sure to pre-iron the fabric to remove any creases or fold lines. Place the dry fabric on the plastic. Dip the 1" brush in the paint and touch the dry fabric with the loaded brush. Apply the paint in a random pattern across the fabric. Allow the paint to migrate into the fabric, then fill in the remaining white areas with the color. Another variation of painting on dry fabric is to spray areas of the dry fabric with water from the spray bottle and then apply paint to the slightly wet areas as well as to the dry areas. This will also give an interesting pattern because of the dilution of the paint in the wet areas.

Using Up Excess Paint

Each fabric type will accept the color differently, so I often paint the same mixed color on a variety of fabrics such as silk twill, silk pongee, and muslin. This results in slightly different values and patterns of the same hue, which can be combined in the projects.

I personally do not like to dispose of any remaining paint, so I try to use up what I have mixed. Often I will wet a piece of muslin with water and pour the small remainders of paint on the muslin. I leave this overnight to dry on plastic. In the morning I am surprised by a beautiful, unique fabric. There is a melange of color, and I use these fabrics in projects, sometimes as the backing of a quilt and sometimes as the focal point of a quilt. (See the Cotton Appliqué Wall Hanging on page 31.)

Overpainting

I use overpainting to enhance a painted background fabric by adding specific colors in certain areas. For best results, overpainting should be done outside in the sun so the second color application will dry quickly. The overpainting can even be added after the quilt or vest has been basted to the batting or foundation fabric, and before any embellishment. (See the Wisteria Vest on page 51.)

Use a 1" paint brush, and drop the paint off the end of the bristles by shaking the brush over the fabric. I prefer to control the size and spacing of the drops, heavy and larger at the top edge, lighter and smaller drops at the bottom edge of a quilt or vest. You can experiment with different spacing for individual projects. Heat set the overpainting again after it has dried by carefully pressing, and avoid stretching or wrinkling the silk.

Spray Painting

Prepare a dilute mixture of approximately one pint of water with two tablespoons of paint, and pour it into a spray bottle. More water or paint can be added to lighten or darken the mixture. Lay the fabric flat on plastic and spray it with the paint mixture. Be careful to protect surrounding surfaces from the spray.

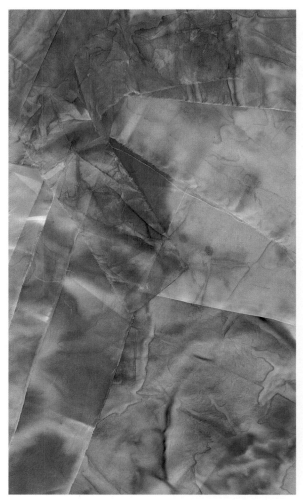

Variety of fabrics

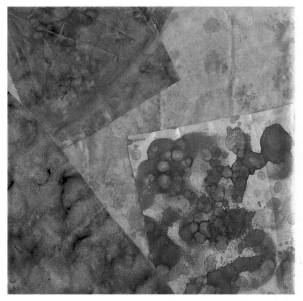

Spray painting

Sun Painting

If the weather permits, fabric can also be painted outside. Spread the dropcloth, or experiment by putting the fabric directly on the lawn. Setacolor is the one fabric paint that offers a heliographic (sun-painting) technique. Quickly paint the whole piece of fabric, then place weeds, flowers, or pre-cut cardboard shapes over the fabric. As it dries, the images will be transferred to the fabric. Interesting results can also come from draping the wet painted fabric over a bush. The images of the leaves will transfer to the fabric. The fabric dries very quickly in the hot sun. The fabric will dry more slowly on a humid day. Heat set the dry fabric. There are many other methods for applying paint to fabric, and just about anything is possible. Experimentation is a lot of fun, and rewarding.

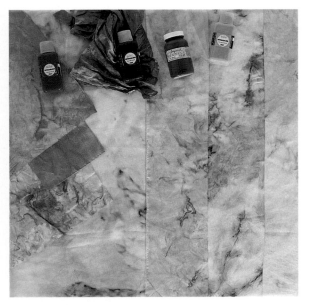

Primary colors (see page 12)

Sponge Painting

Small pieces of a kitchen sponge can be cut into a variety of shapes and used to stamp paint onto the fabric. Cut the sponge while it is dry. Dampen the sponge and squeeze out the excess water. Put a tablespoon of full-strength paint into a disposable aluminum pie pan. Gently press the sponge into the paint to coat the surface with a thin layer of paint, then carefully press the sponge on the fabric. The image of the sponge will be transferred. Continue sponging, re-coating the sponge as needed. Sponge painting can be done in a pattern, or randomly as in the Brenda Doll on page 65 and the Pleated Surface Vest on page 54.

Heat Set the Colors

Fabric paint must be heat set on the fabric to make the color permanent. Always heat set the fabric after it has dried. Use a dry iron on both sides. Remove any wrinkles by spraying with water and ironing again. Do not spray the fabric with water before heat setting the first time, because the water will remove or dilute the color. It is possible to iron the fabric before it is completely dry, provided press cloths are used both over and under the damp fabric. Some of the color will be transferred to the press cloths. Ironing the damp fabric without protection of the ironing surfaces (board and iron) will result in permanent coloring of the ironing board and deposit of paint on the iron.

Caution: Sometimes a noticeable shiny film develops on the back of the dried fabric after it is removed from the dropcloth. This does not damage the fabric, and it is usually caused by a paint mixture that is too thick. It can be prevented by adding more water to the mixture. Carefully heat set the top side of the fabric, using a press cloth underneath to protect the ironing surface. Then wash the fabric in soap and water, which should remove the film. Iron the fabric again.

Secondary colors (see page 12)

Painting Ribbon

Fabric paints can also be used to paint white ribbon. Some of the projects in this book will require painted wire-edged ribbon. These can be painted at the same time you paint your yardage. Lay wide ribbon flat on the dropcloth and apply the color with a paint brush. Narrow silk ribbon can be arranged in a pie pan and painted. Silk ribbon accepts color quickly: just touching the ribbon with a loaded brush is enough to color it. Let the ribbon dry, and heat set it.

Clean-Up

After painting the fabric, clean all brushes and equipment with soap and water. After three or four months of use, the brushes should be cleaned with a brush cleaner (see Resource Guide: Tools) to preserve the bristles. The dropcloth can be wiped with a wet sponge and dried with paper towels. Good maintenance of the dropcloth will allow you to use it many times. For some projects, it is necessary to keep aside a small amount of mixed paint to complete a project or to overpaint certain areas to enhance the design. It is not advisable to keep diluted mixed paint for very long: the minerals and salts in your local water may affect the paint. Small amounts of leftover paint mixtures should be stored in tightly covered glass jars in a dark place. If you store leftover paint, plan to use it soon, or dispose of it after two weeks.

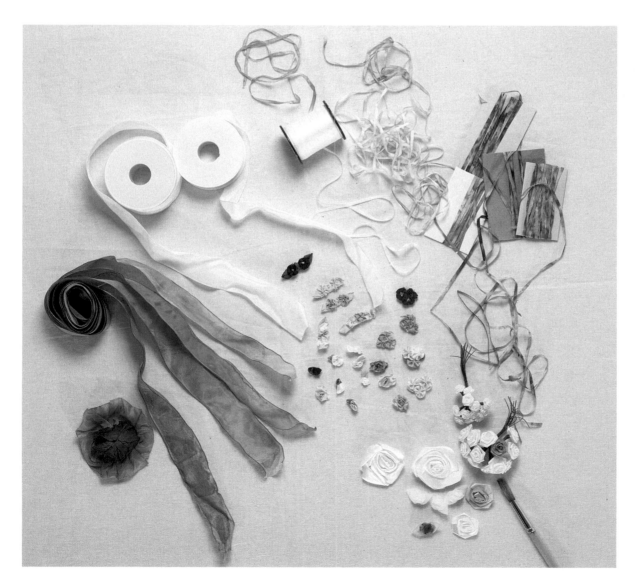

Chapter Three

Sewing & Embellishments

Working with Cotton

Any projects in this book that require painted cotton fabric can be cut and sewn in conventional ways. Cotton can be cut with scissors or with a rotary cutter on a mat. Sewing can be done by hand or machine.

Working with Silk

Silk projects require a few special considerations. Because a cut edge of silk ravels, it is best to handle the silk as little as possible. Pin marks may show in silk, so pins should be as fine as possible, kept to a minimum, and removed as soon as you can. Do not use silk pins, because they are too thick. I recommend extra-fine pleating pins if you can find them. All the silks used for the projects can be torn to provide a measured piece. Be aware that most silks tear only from selvage to selvage, the weft direction. Tear in the warp direction *only* after testing a small piece to see if the edge tears cleanly. To begin a project, select the required yardage and clip the desired amount through the selvage. With a firm grip on either side of the clipped slit, tear the silk towards the opposite selvage. It may be necessary to clip the other selvage to get a clean cut. Each type of silk tears differently, but the technique is not difficult. Silk will drop one or two threads from the torn edge. Clip off these threads and dispose of them, or save them to use. (See the Lyla-san Doll on page 79.)

Thread

It is not necessary to use silk thread when sewing silk fabric. There are many choices; almost any thread is suitable. Try different types of thread, to find the one that works best for you. Matching a thread color to the hand-painted fabric is not difficult. Usually a pastel thread will blend in with watercolor fabrics, darker thread for darker fabrics.

Strip Piecing Silk

Strip piecing is a wonderful technique to use with painted silk: a vest or small quilt can be sewn very quickly. Use a medium-length stitch on the sewing machine and the finest needle. I usually set my Bernina® slightly above the pre-set stitch length, and I use a 60/8 or 70/10 needle. Strip piecing is constructed by sewing strips onto a foundation fabric, and the thread color will not show through the seams if you choose a neutral. Begin by cutting the foundation fabric slightly larger than the pattern for the project. The foundation can be pre-washed and ironed cotton flannel, Fairfield Cotton Classic® batting, polyester batting, or pre-washed and ironed cotton muslin. A flannel or batting foundation gives more dimension to the piecing, while muslin provides a flatter look. Any type of batting could be used as the foundation, provided it will not distort when sewn on the machine. I recommend specific battings in the directions for each project, so you will have an opportunity to try a variety of materials. All the seams will be sewn on the machine and stitched through the silk and the foundation.

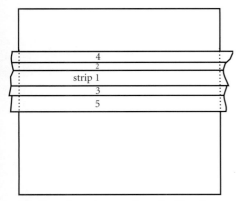

The first strip can be a pre-determined length and placed in the middle of the foundation,

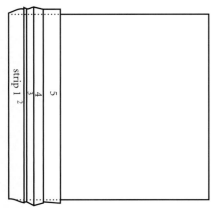

at the edge,

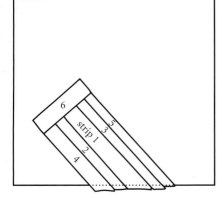

or on the diagonal.

Preparing the Strips

Prepare the silk by tearing eight strips from the painted yardage. Randomly gauge the width of the strips and tear from 1½" to 3" widths, which includes seam allowance. Iron each strip to straighten the torn edge: gently pull the silk with one hand as you guide the iron across the strip. The lengths of the strips will vary with the width of the fabric, since some silk is 35" wide and some 40" or 45". Cut off the selvage before sewing the strips to the foundation. Do not pre-cut the lengths of the strips for your project, because it is easier to trim the lengths after sewing. Begin by placing one strip right side up on the foundation, and pin it in place. The first strip can be a pre-determined length and placed in the middle of the foundation, at the edge, or on the diagonal.

The second strip should not be pre-cut, and it is pinned with right sides together over the first strip, matching up the stitching edge. Pin strip #2 along the edge of #1. Sew along the pinned edge with a ¼" seam allowance. Remove the pins and turn strip #2 right side up; press it flat with a steam iron. Now cut off the extra length from strip #2, making sure you match the top edge with the top edge of strip #1 before trimming. When you iron the sewn strips, it is possible that the strip will slip either up or down so that the top edges are not lined up evenly. Continue piecing across the foundation, sewing each strip and pressing after each seam. It may be necessary to tear more strips to complete the project. Adjust the widths as needed to make a pleasant balance for the strip pieced project. (See the picture below.)

Folded Fabric Overlay (Shown on page 33)

Some projects include a narrow band of color which separates two strips of painted fabric; a folded fabric overlay is an easy method to use. I begin with a full-length strip of painted muslin or silk, 1" or 1½" wide. With a hot iron, I press the strip in half lengthwise, creating a strip ½" or ¾" wide. This strip can be sewn into the seam when you sew two strips together, as in log cabin or strip piecing.

Pin the raw edge of the folded fabric overlay along one edge of a previously pinned strip or square of fabric. Place a second strip over the fabric overlay, giving you four layers of fabric at this pinned edge. Stitch through all layers, turn the second strip right side out, and press. The edge of the folded fabric lies flat against the first strip or square, creating a narrow band of color.

Silk Ribbon Embellishment

Vests

The silk ribbon can be decorative or functional. For a silk vest, the ribbon is a decoration and can be added before the vest is assembled. I position the ribbon by pinning, then sew with a running stitch through the silk and the foundation. The lining for the vest is added after the embellishment.

Quilts

Silk quilts can be decorated with ribbon. Making a quilt with silk is different from sewing with cottons, and you should take some precautions. It is best to test different types of silk before beginning. Basting stitches and pins can permanently mark the silk, so they should be used at a minimum and removed as quickly as possible. I have found that basting the silk top to the batting and the backing often results in unsightly holes on the surface once the basting has been removed.

Silk ribbon offers a way to secure the layers together without basting. I divide the surface of the quilt into quadrants with silk ribbon. Then I pin on the ribbon and sew it to the quilt by stitching through the top, batting, and backing.

I remove the pins as quickly as I stitch. Working on a table with the quilt laid out flat, I put my left hand under the quilt in the area to be sewn and stitch with my right hand. I also stitch the ribbon by stab stitching with the quilt flat on the table. The needle penetrates all the layers and then is brought up again to form a running stitch. Through the years I have not had a problem with this method of sewing. After sewing the ribbon, I add quilting lines one at a time. I do not use a hoop, because the hoop may mark the silk, stretch it, or cause tiny wrinkles. I mark quilting lines with a chalk wheel, carefully pin along the line, and remove the pins as the quilting progresses. Do not leave the pins in place.

Hand Appliqué

There are many wonderful books available on hand appliqué. My method is to work the appliqué fabric as a single layer. I draw my design on paper, make a plastic template from the drawing, draw template shapes on the fabric and, when cutting out the design, I add a seam allowance. The drawn line serves as my stitching line and I clip the edges of the appliqué where necessary before I begin sewing. I pin the pieces to the background fabric; large appliqué pieces are basted to the background to secure the shapes before stitching by hand. (See page 33.)

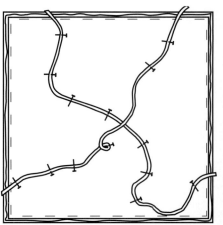

Layer the batting and backing with silk on top. Baste around edges. Divide into quadrants and pin on silk ribbon.

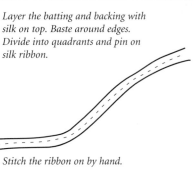

Stitch the ribbon on by hand.

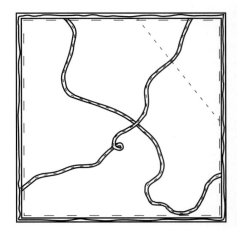

Mark quilting lines one at a time with chalk. Carefully pin along line, and remove pins as quilting progresses. Do not leave pins in place.

Burned Silk Appliqué

Touch the side of the flame with the silk. ➡

One of the most exciting methods of appliqué is burned silk, which does not require turning under the raw edges. The silk is shaped by burning the edges. Each type of silk burns differently, and I recommend you use only the types suggested in this book. Burning a very heavy silk does not give a pleasing result. Lightweight silks (less than 12mm) are best. There is an odor from burning silk, so prepare to do the burning outside or in a room with very good ventilation.

Burning Silk

The technique is very easy and, with a little practice, can result in some wonderful shapes. You will need a dripless candle in a good sturdy holder, matches, two old towels, and a bucket of water. The water may not be necessary, but it is a good precaution. If the burning accelerates, drop the silk into the water. Additional precaution would be to set the candle holder in an aluminum pie pan and put water in the pie pan.

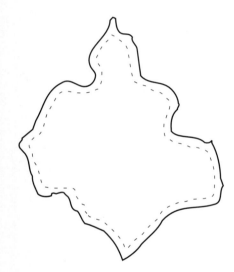

Prepare all the fabrics to be burned before lighting the candle. For some shapes, a strip of torn silk can be used; for others, it will be necessary to cut pieces of silk. Small pieces should be handled with a clamp or pliers, so that your fingers do not get too close to the flame.

Touch the side of the flame with the silk, using an in-and-out motion to bring the fabric close to the side of the flame and out again to control the burning. The silk strip can be cut by using the edge of the flame. Pull carefully on both sides of where you want the cut, as you touch the silk to the flame. This is the method I use for making leaf shapes. I pull the silk so the flame travels across the strip and makes an interesting cut. I re-burn the edges to get the leaf shape. It takes a little practice, but after a few tries you should be getting the desired shapes.

Cautions: There are a few tips to remember when you use this technique. Do not put the silk near the top of the flame, because this will smoke the silk and color it with soot. Do not touch the silk to the wax, because the wax will burn very quickly, destroy your shape, and possibly burn the silk in your hand. Drop the silk into the water if it touches the wax, then begin with a new piece of silk. Do not shake the piece of silk if the edge is still burning. Blow with your mouth to put out any smoldering area. If you shake the silk, tiny beads of melting silk could stick to your hand.

Cleaning the Burned Silk Edges

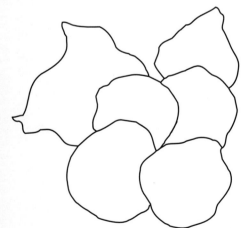

After burning the shapes, you must clean the charcoal from the edges. These don't look like much, but they will cause a mess if they are not rubbed off. Place two old towels on the work surface. Put a few burned shapes on one towel and rub the edges with your finger; turn the shapes over and rub again. Transfer the shapes to the clean towel. Shake the debris from the first towel as needed. It may be necessary to clean the edges again on the second towel if you did not rub them off enough the first time. This takes a little time; I am always impatient with this process, because I want to put the shapes on my silk background to see how wonderful they look. But do take the time to clean the edges first. You may still have to blow away a bit of the burned edge as you begin to stitch, if the edge is loosened. Remarkably, this technique is very stable. I have used it for over twelve years, and I have never had a problem with the appliqué.

Sewing the Burned Silk

The appliqué is stitched by hand to the project. A running stitch just inside the burned edge is enough to secure the piece to the background.

As you build up the design, it may be necessary to layer the shapes. Sew the top shape to secure the one on the bottom.

Foundation Fabric

Foundation fabrics for blocks, quilts, and garments can be cotton flannel, cotton muslin, or a variety of battings. For clothing, I suggest a thin foundation such as Cotton Classic, or a polyester batting such as Low Loft® or Thermore®, cotton muslin, or flannel. Pre-wash muslin or flannel and iron before using it in any of the projects. Cotton Classic batting can be gently rinsed and dried for easier handling. Fill a washing machine 1/3 full, unfold the batting, and remove any paper. Gently ease the batting into the water, pushing down carefully to wet the batting. Do not agitate, but spin the water out of the machine and carefully lift the wet batting into the dryer. Dry on normal setting. After the batting has dried it can be steamed to remove any wrinkles. Do not touch the iron directly onto batting: put a press cloth over the batting and lightly press, or hold the iron 1" above the batting and allow the steam to penetrate the batting. Smooth out wrinkles with your hand. It is not necessary to rinse a polyester batting, but it can also be steamed as just described to remove wrinkles.

Tools for Trimming

Use a rotary cutter and mat on all edges, to trim excess fabric and when cutting cotton fabrics. Most silk fabrics for the projects will be torn into manageable strips and trimmed with the rotary cutter. A general-width plastic ruler can be used with the rotary cutter, such as an Omnigrid® 6" by 24".

Seam Allowance

All seams are sewn with a ¼" allowance. Use a walking foot on the sewing machine when sewing though multiple layers of fabric and batting. This foot evenly feeds the top and bottom layers and prevents bunching and movement of the layers.

Seam Binding

Finish all raw edges with a binding unless otherwise stated. The binding can be cut from painted fabrics in contrasting or matching colors. All straight-edge seams use a straight grain binding; all curved seams use a bias binding. All binding is cut 1½" wide and sewn with a ¼" seam allowance unless specified otherwise. Pin the binding right sides together to the project top, matching raw edges, and stitch. Press the binding out and fold in the raw edge to meet the raw edge of the seam. Fold the binding again and pin it in place over the seam, then slipstitch the folded edge of the binding over the seam line.

Quilt Sleeve

A quilt sleeve is a folded fabric casing added to the top edge of the back of the quilt and used to hang the quilt. The sleeve extends the length of the top of the quilt and should be deep enough to accept a hanging rod. It is made in two pieces, with an opening at the center.

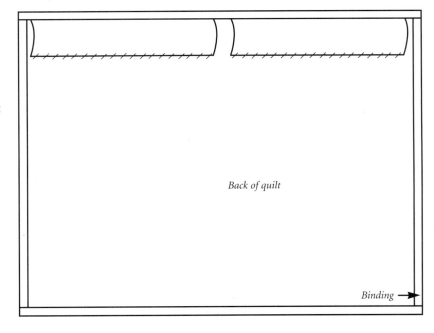

Back of quilt

Binding →

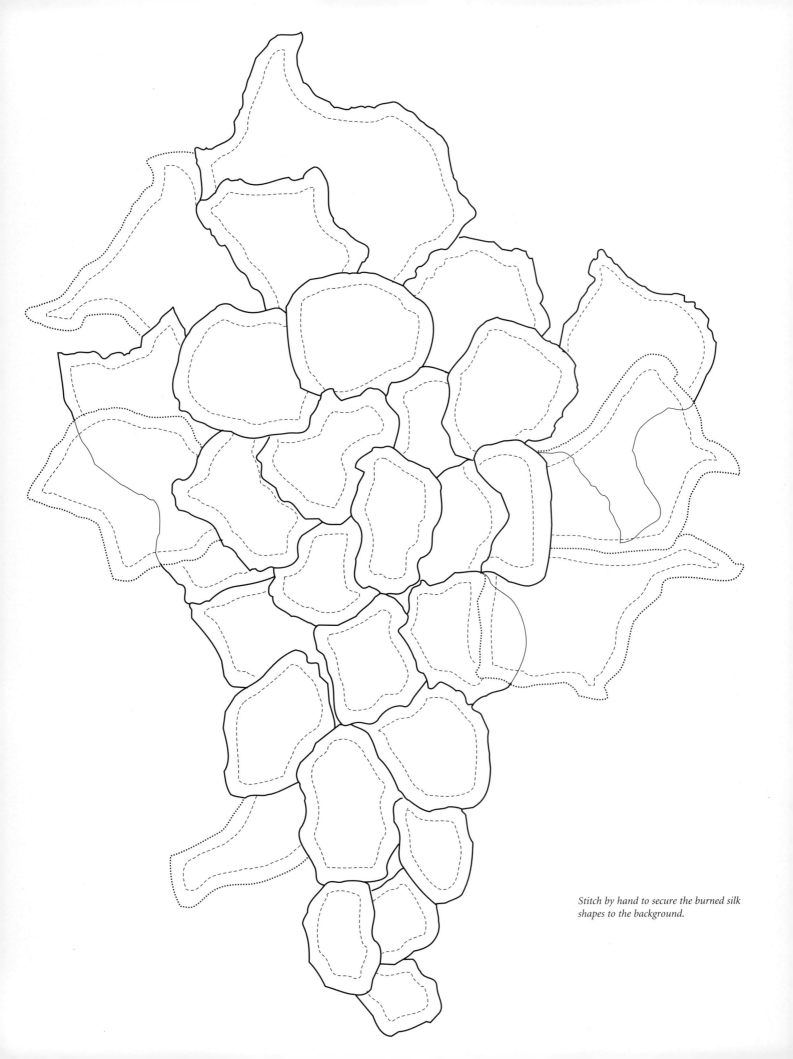

*Stitch by hand to secure the burned silk
shapes to the background.*

Chapter Four

Quilts, Blocks, & Wall Hangings

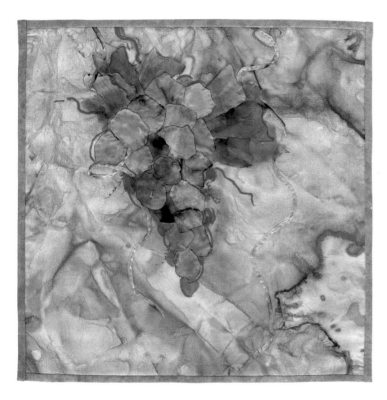

Burned Silk Appliqué Grapes

This sample block uses three colors and three different types of silk. The block is sewn by hand using burned silk appliqué.

Fabric Requirements

- ◆ Gold pongee: 14" x 14"
- ◆ Purple silk twill: 1¾" full-width strip cut into nineteen squares
- ◆ Green silk twill: 3" full-width strip
- ◆ Green silk organza: 3" full-width strip
- ◆ Gold silk ribbon, 3.8 mm: 12"
- ◆ Purple silk ribbon, 3.8 mm: 24"
- ◆ Muslin: 15" x 15"

Lay the gold pongee over the muslin, pin along the four edges, baste, then remove the pins. Burn the edges of cut squares of purple silk to make nineteen grapes. Burn six leaves each from the green twill and green organza strip: be careful, because organza burns very quickly! Clean off the burned edges on the shapes. Layer the leaves on the gold pongee and place the purple grapes over the leaves. Arrange the circles to look like a grape cluster by overlapping some of the shapes.

Pin all the shapes in place and begin stitching by hand to secure the silk to the gold background. Arrange the silk ribbon to complement the grape cluster, pin it in place, and secure it with a running stitch in the center of the ribbon.

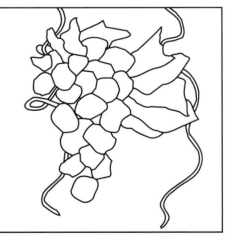

Arrange circles to look like a grape cluster by overlapping some of the shapes.

Strip Piecing, Log Cabin Style

This sample block features two colors painted on muslin and on different types of silk. Strips of various widths are pieced to a quilt batting. The sample features Low Loft polyester batting. Various types of batting affect the finished block. A flat batting, such as flannel or muslin, does not offer much density to the quilt, and quilting stitches would look very flat, whereas a thicker batt would create a fuller look. It is a good idea, when beginning to work with a new technique, to test a variety of battings. Compare the photo on page 24, which is strip pieced to flannel: notice the different results.

Fabric Requirements

- ◆Orange and blue silk twill, pongee, and spun silk: eight to ten torn full-width silk strips, 1" to 3" wide
- ◆Blue muslin (cut with rotary cutter): 4" square and 1½" x 45" strip
- ◆Batting: 15" x 15" square of Low Loft

Sewing the Block

Trim the selvage from the muslin and silk strips. Place a 4" muslin square on the batting and pin it on all four sides. Place a strip of silk on the top and bottom edge of the square, right sides together. Pin it in place and stitch. Trim off the excess strip length, then fold out the strips and iron them carefully: do not touch the batting with the iron. Repeat on the two other sides of the square, alternating the widths of the strips. Sew two strips at a time, and iron.

Cover all the batting to finish the 15" square. Trim the edges with a rotary cutter to make a 14½" square.

Begin piecing around the center square #1. Follow diagram for suggested placement of remaining strips until block is covered with sewn strips.

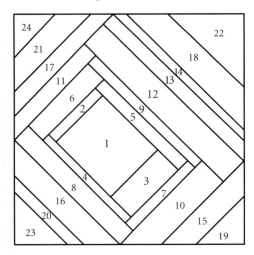

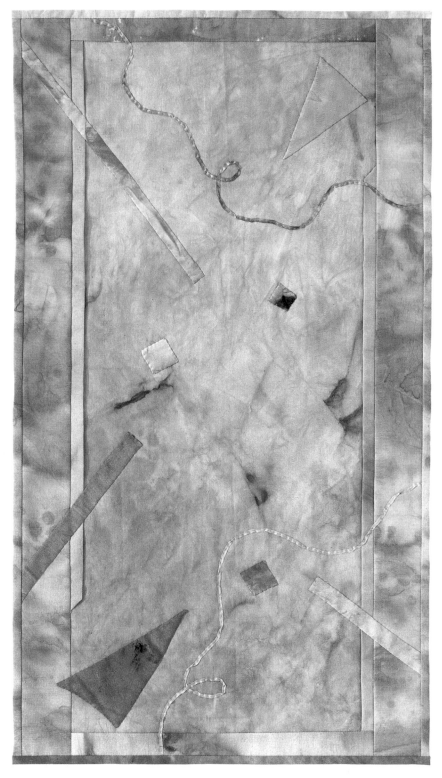

Cotton Appliqué Wall Hanging

17" x 31"

This project can be made with different proportions and colors of cotton fabrics for the pieced background and the appliqué shapes. The sample quilt features a painted muslin center panel and strips decorated with silk appliqué triangles, bars, and squares, and silk ribbon. The center panel was painted with leftover paint—pink, green, buttercup, gold, and blue for the melange; taupe, tan, rust, green, gold with Bengal pink drops, cobalt blue, dilute velvet brown with ultramarine and gold, emerald, and Parma violet. (See Using Up Excess Paint on page 19.)

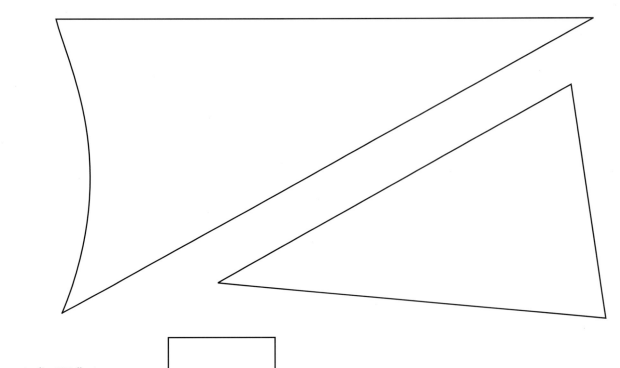

Patterns for Cotton Appliqué Wall Hanging (add ¼" seam allowance)

Fabric Requirements

◆ Muslin: melange of color for center panel 13" x 29"
gold and pink, 9" x 45", cut into two strips 2½" x 45" and two strips 1½" x 45"
brown and blue/gold, one strip of each, 1½" x 13"
tan 1½" x 13", 1½" x 18", and 18" x 32"
blue, two strips 1½"x 24" folded and ironed to ¾" x 24"

◆ Gold pongee: 1½" x 18"

◆ Cotton flannel batting: 18" x 32"

◆ Gold silk 3.8 mm ribbon: 26"

◆ Green silk 3.8 mm ribbon: 26"

◆ Silk fabrics for appliqué:
Pongee: blue 1½" x 7"
taupe 1½" x 9"
rust 1½" x 13"
tan triangle 3" x 4¼"
green triangle 3½" x 6½"
Silk twill: green, purple, and gold 2" squares

Sewing the Patchwork

Begin by centering the 13" x 29" muslin on the flannel and pin it in place. Pin the folded ¾" x 24" blue muslin folded fabric overlay on the left and right edges of the center panel, matching up the raw edges. (See Folded Fabric Overlay on page 25.) Place the folded strip at the top edge on the left side and bottom edge of the right side. Fold under the short end to form a triangle, as shown:

COLORS CHANGING HUE

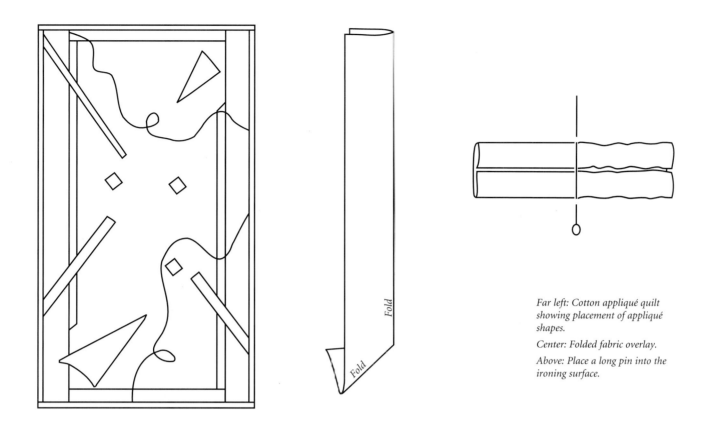

Pin, with right sides together, the blue/gold on the top and brown strips on the bottom of the center panel. Machine stitch through the flannel, then press the strips out. Pin the 2½" x 31" gold and pink strips face down over the folded blue muslin on the left and right sides of the center panel. Stitch through all layers and press the strips out. Press the pieced top and layer it with the muslin backing fabric, wrong sides together, with the flannel in the middle. Pin and baste along the four edges.

Appliqué

Fold the blue, taupe, and rust strips with the raw edges to the back. An easy method to fold short strips accurately is to place a long pin into the ironing surface, pull the folded silk through the center of the pin, and iron it as it is pulled through.

Use the patterns for templates to cut out the triangles and squares. Fold over the seam allowance and iron. Pin and then stitch the appliqué shapes in place, along with the ribbon, and stitch. Trim the edges of the quilt to 17" x 31" with a rotary cutter. For this small wall hanging, use a single-fold 1½" binding to cover the raw edges. (See Seam Binding on page 27.) Use the gold with pink muslin strips to bind the left and right sides, tan to bind the top, and gold pongee to bind the bottom. Put a sleeve at the top edge of the quilt for hanging. (See Quilt Sleeve on page 27.)

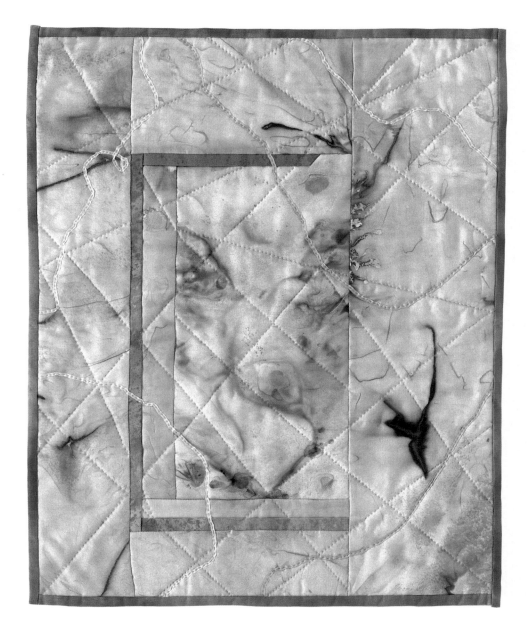

Rose and Green Silk Small Quilt

19"x 24"

This sample has some special painted fabrics that resulted from experimentation. I used a small, beautiful scrap of painted silk for the center panel and wide bands of unusual silk for the borders. The center panel was part of a one-yard piece that I painted Bengal pink on one half and emerald on the other. While the fabric was wet, I splashed a few drops of pink over the emerald, and emerald over the pink. The design was not planned, but when the fabric dried the spots of pink looked like rosebuds. I cut this portion out to use as the center panel and edged it with the emerald-speckled pink. The border fabric was painted with a mixture of Bengal pink and a dash of black, with about one tablespoon of pearl white iridescent paint. The paints were mixed in a large basin, but some of the white was not completely blended in. One yard of silk twill was folded, submerged, and left for about three hours, then opened out and laid flat to dry. Unlikely to duplicate this exact design, I decided to make a small quilt to remind me of the spontaneous color effect. You can try any color combination and different methods of painting.

Fabric Requirements

- ◆ Silk twill: emerald with pink 7½" x 14½" center panel
  pink with emerald spots 2⅜" x 14½" and 1¾" x 9⅜" strips
  pink with black and pearl white 1 yard border fabric
- ◆ Muslin: emerald 1½" full-width strip cut with rotary cutter
  for fabric overlay, folded to ¾", then cut to 9⅜", 8", and 16"
  green with tan for backing 21" x 26"
- ◆ Flannel: 21" x 26"
- ◆ Green silk 3.8 mm ribbon: 1 yard
- ◆ White silk 3.8 mm ribbon: 1½ yards

Making the Quilt

Lay the cotton flannel on the table and position the center silk panel 6½" from the left edge and 7" from the right edge, 6" from the top and 5½" from the bottom; pin along the edges. Pin, right sides together, the 2⅜" x 14½" strip of pink-emerald twill on to the left edge of the center panel; stitch and press out. Pin the 1¾" x 9⅜" strip of pink-emerald twill to the lower edge of the panel; stitch and press out. Pin the 9⅜" folded emerald muslin strip, raw edges together, to the bottom strip. Pin the 8" folded emerald muslin strip to the top edge, then fold under the right end of the strip to make a triangle. Pin the 16" folded emerald muslin strip to the left edge of the center panel. Tear two strips from the pink fabric to use for borders, 6½" and 4½" widths. Use the rotary cutter to cut a 24" and a 10" length from each strip. Tear the 10" strips to 3½" and 5½" widths to use as directed. (This allows for some loss of width during tearing.) Press the torn strips before sewing and trim the lengths to 9⅜". Pin the 3½" x 9⅜" strip to the bottom panel edge and stitch all layers, then press out. Pin the 5½" x 9⅜" strip to the top panel edge and stitch all layers, then press out. Pin the 4½" x 24" strip to the left edge, stitch through all layers, then press out. Pin the 6½" x 24" strip to the right edge, stitch through all layers, then press out.

Quilting and Finishing

Put the muslin backing, wrong sides together, next to the flannel. Pin the layers together and baste along the edges. Pin the ribbon over the quilt surface, as shown, and stitch by hand.

Draw a diagonal line with a chalk wheel and quilt along the line. Continue drawing and quilting until the surface is covered with random lines.

After quilting, trim the quilt to measure 19" x 24" and finish the edges with a 1½" single-fold binding of your choice, to co-ordinate with the quilt. (See Seam Binding on page 27.) Add a sleeve for hanging the quilt. (See Quilt Sleeve on page 27.)

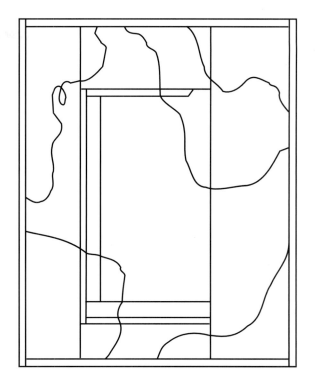

Placement of ribbons over surface

Chalk lines

Summer Bouquet Silk Quilt

25½" x 35½"

The beauty of this quilt comes from a variety of flower shapes and colors applied over a pale silk background. Narrow strips of eighteen different colors are used for the flowers. You can experiment with color mixtures for your flowers, since burned silk flowers are not realistic.

The technique for making this quilt is to layer a pale iridescent gold background fabric over the batting and the backing. Wire-edged ribbon, silk organza, and silk ribbons are sewn over the background, through the batting and backing, before the flowers are added.

Fabric Requirements

- Gold silk twill: 26" x 36"
- Gold muslin: 1½ yards, for backing and binding
- Batting: Cotton Classic, Low Loft, or Thermore 26" x 36"
- Silk twill for flowers and leaves:
  orange 2½" strip: burn six petals
  pale orange 1" strip: burn seven oval petals
  dark gold 2" strip: burn six petals
  gray with gold 2" strip, cut into 1" squares: burn fourteen round petals
  white 2" strip: burn five petals
  pale cobalt 1" strip: burn seven round petals
  pale ultramarine 1" strip: burn four round petals
  dark purple 1½" strip: burn ten petals
  light purple 3" strip: burn seven petals
  periwinkle 2" strip: burn five petals
  green 2" strip: burn four petals
  taupe 1¾" strip: burn seven round petals
  pomegranate 2" strip: burn three round shapes
  red bud 1" strip: burn four elliptical shapes
  dark green 1" and 3" strips: burn twelve leaves
- Silk organza sheer for leaves:
  gold 3½" strip: burn seven leaves
  rust 3½" strip: burn four leaves
  burgundy 3½" strip: burn five leaves
  dark green 1" and 3" strips: burn twelve leaves
  dark green 1¾" and 1½" full-width strips for background
- Gold silk 3.8 mm ribbon: 5 yards
- Green silk 3.8 mm ribbon: 1½ yards
- Gold wire-edged ribbon, 1½" and 1" wide: one yard each

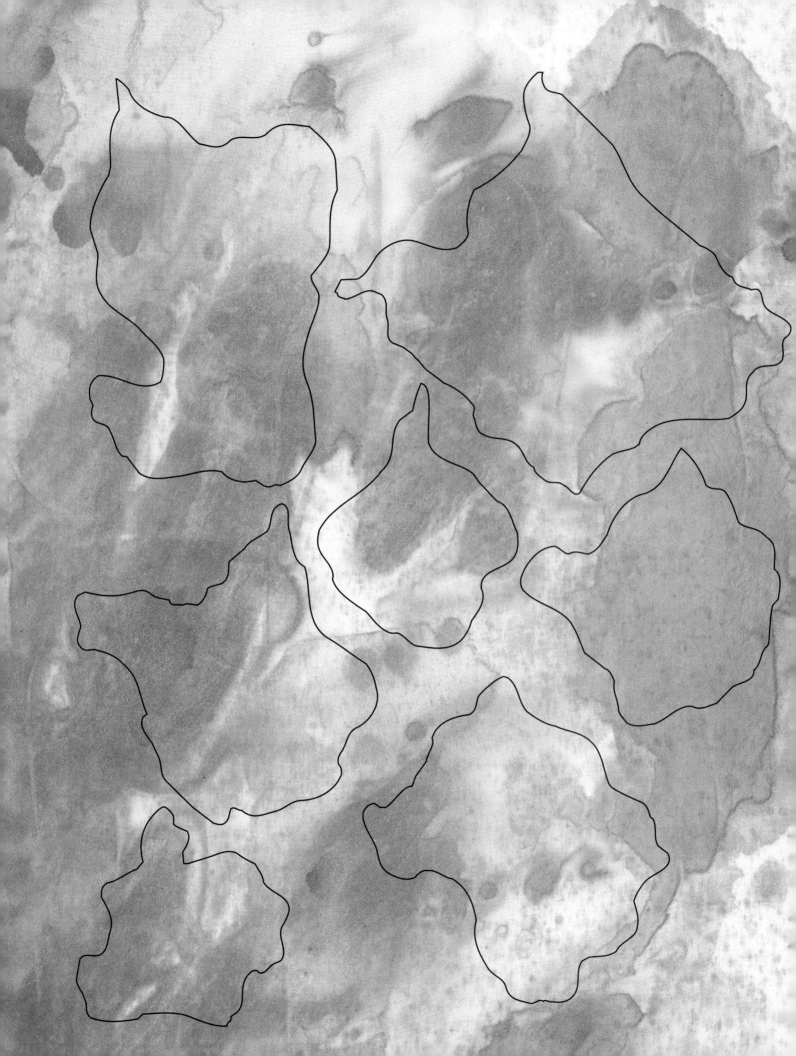

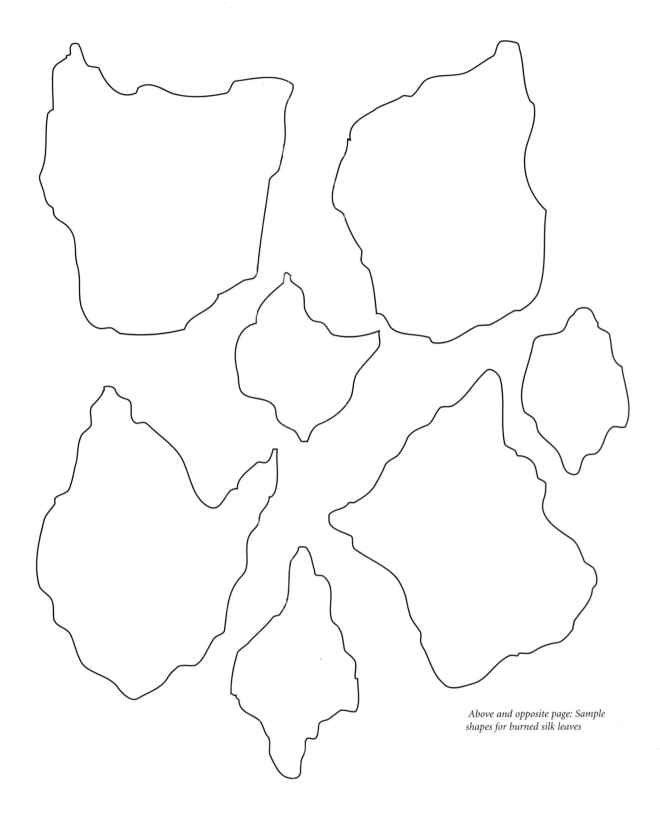

Above and opposite page: Sample shapes for burned silk leaves

Burning the Flower and Leaf Shapes

Prepare the flower and leaves by burning the shapes. (Shapes found on pages 38 and above.)

Cover a tray with a towel, and stack the petals and leaves by color on the tray. Clean off the burned edges.

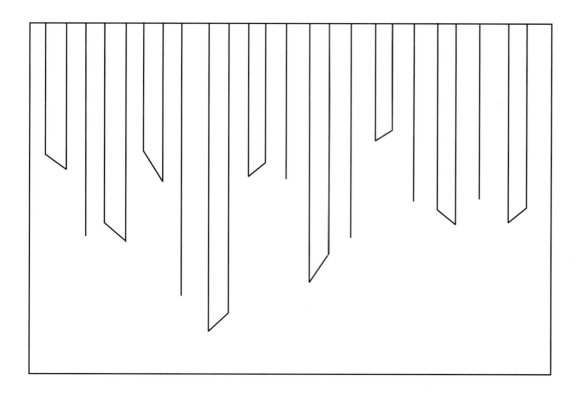

Preparing the Background of the Quilt

Lay the backing fabric on the table, wrong side up, and position the batting over the backing. Place the gold silk twill on top and match the edges. Pin around the edges and baste.

Burn the dark green organza 1¾" and 1½" strips along the edges to remove any ravels. Hold the strip near the edge of the flame and do not allow the flame to burn into the strip. Cut the strips into five lengths (18", 10", 20", 23", 12") and trim one end of each to a 45° angle. Cut the 1½" and 1" wire-edged ribbon into four lengths (19", 16", 12", 17") and trim one end of each to a 45° angle. Cut the gold and green silk ribbon into six lengths (14½", 15", 18", 17", 20", 16") and trim one end of each to a 45° angle.

Sewing Ribbons and Organza to the Background

Space them in a pattern over the quilt, alternating widths and colors. Draw straight lines on the quilt with a chalk wheel. Pin the ribbons and organza, beginning from the right edge, matching the straight cut edge with the top edge of the quilt.

Stitch by hand, trying to make the stitches go through to the backing fabric.

Arranging the Flowers and Leaves

After all the ribbons have been stitched, it is time to arrange the flowers and leaves. Form a pattern across the lower edge of the quilt. (See page 43.)

It is easiest to lay out some of the leaves first, to establish the edges of the design, then place the petals over the leaves. Tuck more leaves under the petals to cover up most of the background fabric. Use different colors of leaves to enhance the colors of the flowers. Sometimes it is necessary to move a flower or leaves for a more pleasing design. Pin the shapes in place and stitch. Some edges can be left open, but secure most to the quilt, so there is a uniformity to the stitching. (If some edges are open, be careful not to crease these shapes when you transport or store the quilt.) While you are stitching the flowers, some of the burned edges may still come loose. Just blow them off the quilt as you are stitching.

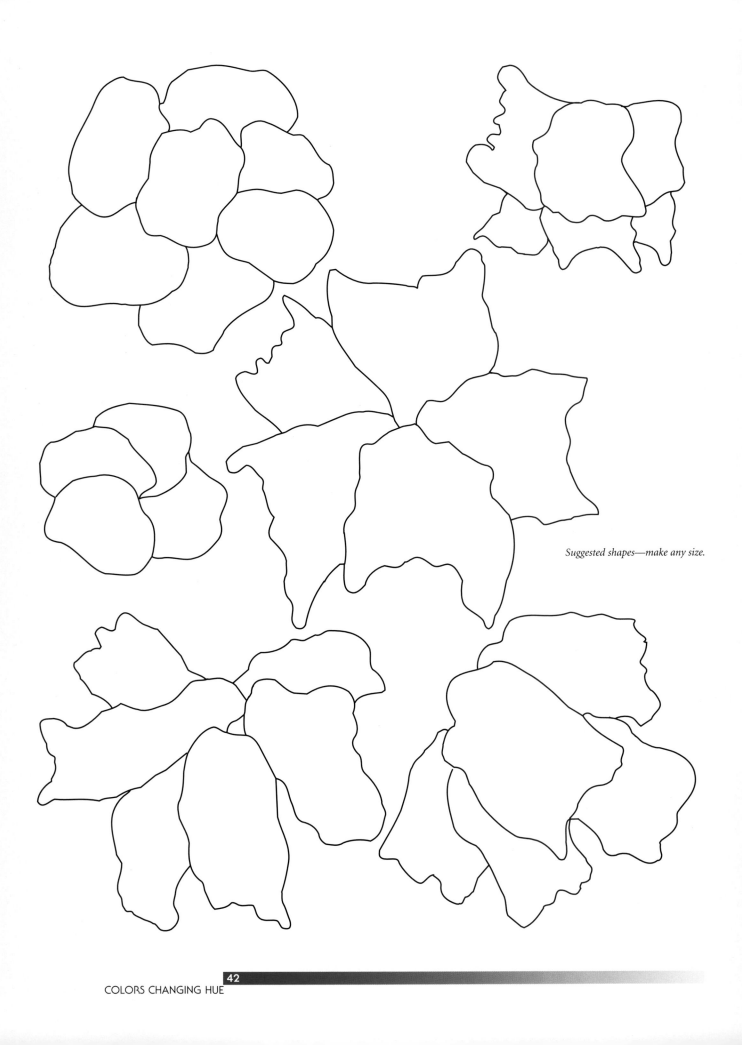

Suggested shapes—make any size.

COLORS CHANGING HUE

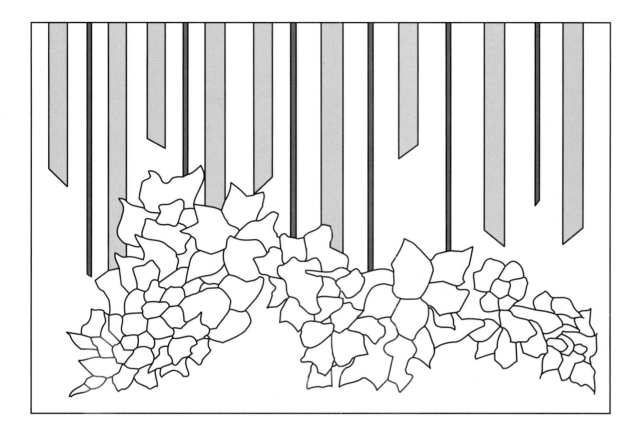

Sewing the Silk Ribbon

Arrange the remaining 3½ yards of gold silk ribbon across the surface of the quilt, pin, then stitch.

Double tack stitch the ribbon ¼" in from the edges to secure it. When the quilt is trimmed, the ends of the ribbon will be secured by the binding.

Finishing the Quilt

Trim the edges of the quilt with the rotary cutter to 25½" x 35½". From the remaining gold muslin, cut binding strips long enough to cover the edges of the quilt, and a sleeve for hanging. The painted muslin will make a nice contrast on the edges.

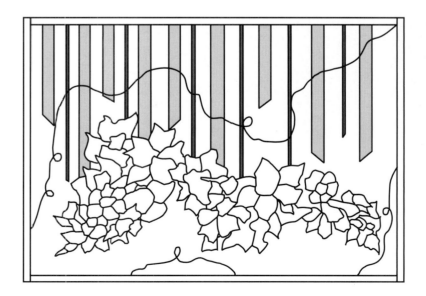

COLORS CHANGING HUE

Chapter Five

Vests

Vest with Armhole Band

I designed this vest pattern in 1975, and it continues to be a favorite of mine. The directions first appeared in my book *Five Ethnic Patterns*, which was published in 1977, and a slightly altered version appeared in *Pieced Clothing* in 1980. The flat pattern pieces which include center fronts, center back, side panels, and armhole bands are easy to piece, appliqué, or embellish. The lower edge of the vest is curved to a point in the center front and back, and binding is used to trim and assemble the vest.

Instructions for two different variations of this vest feature silk machine strip piecing and hand appliqué burned silk. This has an additional embellishment called overpainting. (See Overpainting on page 19.)

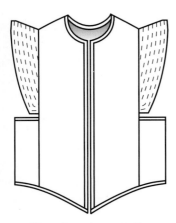

The neck opening, center front edges, lower edge, and top of side panels are covered with seam binding.

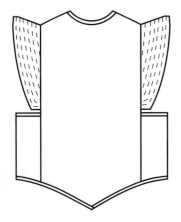

General Directions for Vest Construction

Altering the Vest Pattern

A size medium vest pattern is inserted in the back of the book. The flat pattern shapes can be altered to fit different sizes. If you need to adjust the pattern for a smaller or larger size, use the following directions. Measure your bust measurement and add at least 2" for ease. Look in a mirror to determine the width of your center panel by holding the tape measure from inside armhole to inside armhole. The center front and back panels are the same width, so combine the two and subtract that number from the adjusted bust measurement. Divide the remaining number in half to determine the width of each side panel at the top under-arm edge. The length of the vest in center front and back is 6" below the waist, and it curves up 3" below the waist at the side edge. For some sizes, the hip measurement width at 3" below the waist is larger than the adjusted bust measurement, so it may be necessary to add to the width of the lower edge of the side panel. Measure your hip measurement, then subtract the center panel measurements plus the side panels; half of the remaining number should be added to the width of each side panel at the lower edge. In some cases, the side panel is slightly angled out at the lower edge to accommodate this change in size. Depth of the armhole is 10½" from the shoulder. Subtract the length of the armhole depth from the length of the center panel to determine the length of the side panel. Add or subtract your measurements to the pattern and add seam allowance to all pieces before cutting. The neck opening, center front edges, lower edge, and top of side panels are covered with seam binding.

Foundation Fabric and Lining

All the pattern pieces are cut from a cotton flannel foundation fabric. This foundation can be cut slightly larger than the pattern and trimmed to the correct size after the piecing or appliqué, when you cut the lining. My method for cutting the lining in tandem with the trimming of the patchwork eliminates the problem of trying to match up the raw edges of the lining with the patchwork, especially helpful when working with slippery silk lining fabric. Piece or embellish all the vest pattern pieces on the foundation fabric, then prepare the lining. Layer the pieced or embellished pattern pieces by placing them wrong sides together over the lining fabric. Pin the layers together and place the vest pattern on top of the patchwork pieces. Trim them to the correct size with a rotary cutter. Pin again along the cut edges. This method guarantees a clean edge to all the layers, which will be sewn with a ¼" seam allowance.

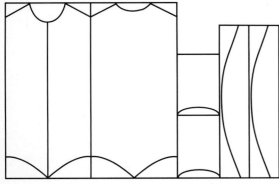

Pattern layout for vest with armhole band

Binding the Center Front

Finish the center front edges with straight grain binding to secure this edge and eliminate raveling. Cut two strips of muslin 1½" x 45", or tear two 1½" strips of silk and use them to bind the front edges. Pin the binding to the center left and right edges, matching the raw edges, and stitch. Press the binding over the seam and fold in the raw edge of the binding to meet the raw edge of the seam. Fold the binding again and pin it over the seam line. Slipstitch the folded edge of the binding over the seam line. Trim the binding even with the top front edge of the neck opening and the lower front edge.

Shoulder and Neck Edge

To finish the shoulder seams, sew all three layers of the center back, including the lining, to two layers of the center front excluding the lining. Press the seam toward the center front and hand sew the front panel lining over the shoulder seam. Finish the neck edge with a 1½" strip of bias binding. Sew the bias binding around the neck edge and leave ½" of the binding extended beyond the center front edges of the neck opening. Press binding over the seam, fold in the extra ½" binding on the front edges, and fold binding again and pin over the seam line. Slipstitch the folded edge over the seam line and stitch the front edge fold.

Side Panels

Finish the top edge of the side panels with straight grain binding which is left over from the center panel front edge binding.

Armhole Bands

Armhole bands are three layers: cut two bands for the outside, two bands for the lining, and two flannel. Begin by pinning the flannel to the wrong side of the outside fabric bands along all the edges, then baste around the edges. With right sides together, layer the armhole lining over the outside band and pin along the curved edge and both ends. Stitch along the curved edge and across the ends with ¼" seam allowance.

Carefully clip the curved edge, turn the band to the outside, and press. Line up the straight edge of the armhole bands and pin along this edge and across the surface. Top stitch every ⅜".

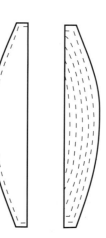

Armhole band. Stitch along the curved edge.

Topstitch armhole band.

Assembling the Vest

Sew the armhole bands and the side panels to the center panel fronts and back with bias binding over the seams. With right sides together, pin the straight edge of the armhole band to the center panel front and back, matching up the center of the band with the shoulder seam. Right sides together, pin the side panels to the center panels by matching the lower curved edges. Sew the seam with the bias binding to assemble the vest. Do *not* sew the seam twice (once to assemble and once to put on the binding): sew the seam *with* the binding on top of armhole band and side panels. Press this binding over the seam to the lining side and press the seam again on the outside of the vest. Turn the vest to the inside and fold in the raw edge of the binding. It will be necessary to clip the edges of the seam at the shoulder edge, to allow the seam to be turned flat against the center panel.

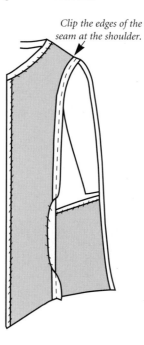

Clip the edges of the seam at the shoulder.

Slipstitch the binding to the lining fabric of the center panel as shown, being careful the stitches do not show on the outside of the vest.

Finishing the Lower Edge

Press the vest again and finish the lower curved edge with 1½" bias binding. Allow an extra ¾" binding at the right center front edge. On the outside of the vest, stitch the bias binding from the right center front edge just to the center point of the back. Fold in the ¾" extra binding at the right front edge to make a nice point, trim if necessary, press the binding, and slipstitch in place. Cut off the binding at the center back even with the point. Now allow another extra ¾" of binding at the center back and continue stitching the binding around to the left center front; leave ¾" extra. Fold in, arrange, and clip the center back binding to make a neat point. Clip the excess binding if necessary and do the same on the left front. Press the binding and slipstitch it in place. Slipstitch the edge folds.

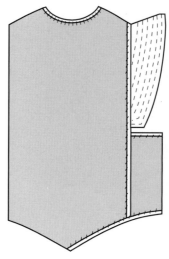

Strip Pieced Vest with Armhole Band

Any cotton or silk fabric is suitable to use for the strip piecing on this vest. The sample vest is made with blue and peach silk twill. If you choose to use cottons for the strip piecing, cut the strips with a rotary cutter; silk fabrics are torn into strips. (See Strip Piecing Silk on page 23.) The triangle ornaments inserted in the patchwork seams are called prairie points. The tips of these triangles are tacked with a small piece of silk ribbon. The vest requires three yards of silk twill painted with different color combinations: one yard indigo with white areas and peach accents, one yard peach with indigo, and one yard an overall mix of peach and indigo. Prairie points are made from another scrap of previously painted fabric which has white, blue, yellow, and ultramarine.

Fabric Requirements

(for medium size)

- Silk twill: one yard each of indigo with white and peach, peach with indigo, and mixed peach and indigo, for piecing and lining
  multicolored 3" full-width strip cut into twelve squares 3" x 3" for prairie points
- Indigo muslin: ½ yard for binding
- Flannel: one yard for foundation
- Pale blue silk 3.8 mm ribbon: 1½ yards

Prairie Points

Cut twelve squares from the multicolored 3" strip. Press the squares in half and fold down the right and left edges of the fold to meet in the middle, creating a folded triangle. Press again. Put these aside to be used in the strip piecing.

Strip Piecing

Cut the pattern pieces from cotton flannel and sew the torn silk strips to the back panel. (See the directions for Preparing the Strips on page 24.) I always begin patchwork or appliqué on any vest on the back panel first. This is the largest pattern piece; it seems appropriate to work to the smaller pieces. The patchwork begins with a large triangle; the strips are added until the pattern piece is covered.

Add prairie points in the seams. Press each seam after sewing. Continue piecing center fronts and side panels. (See General Directions for Vest Construction on page 46 to assemble the vest.)

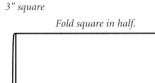

3" square

Fold square in half.

Fold down right and left edges of top to meet in the middle.

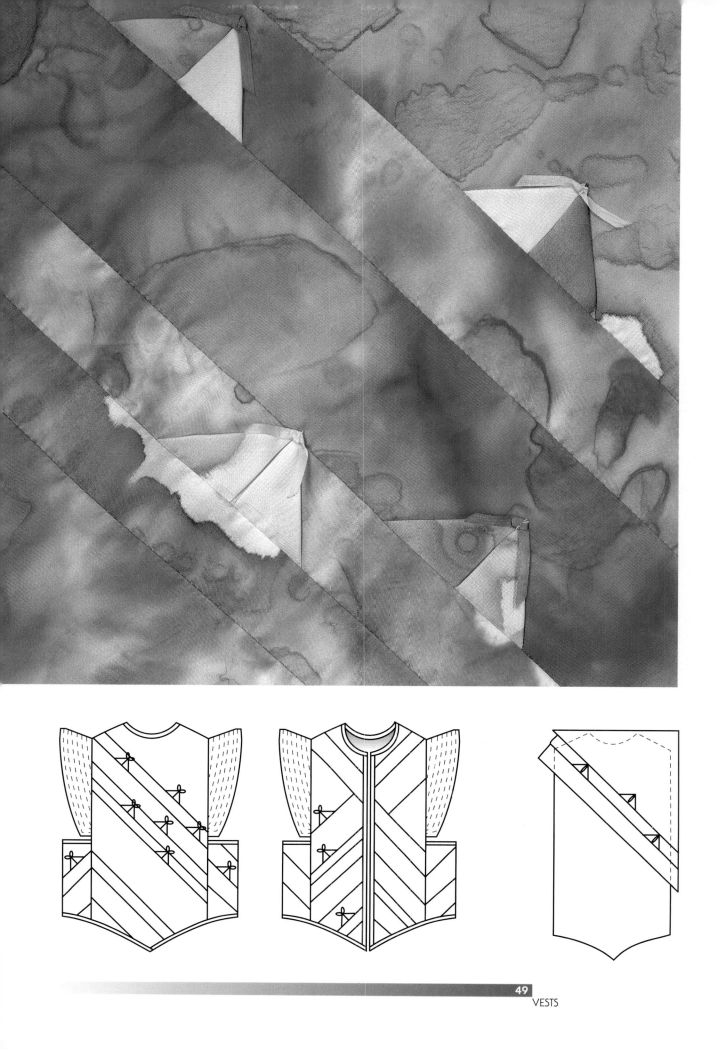

Wisteria Vest with Burned Silk Appliqué

This project features overpainting with burned silk appliqué. The background fabric was spray painted in pale gray. (See Spray Painting on page 19.) I used one yard of suèded silk for the sample vest. This silk is very tightly woven, and the paint beads up on the surface; it takes a few minutes for the paint to penetrate. You can substitute phoenix pongee for the suèded silk. After heat setting the first color application, baste the vest pattern pieces to the flannel foundation fabric.

Layering the Silk Over the Foundation

An easy way to baste the silk and foundation together is to lay the silk over the flannel and trace the pattern pieces onto the silk. Use a very fine permanent pen or a chalk wheel to mark the cutting lines. Baste around all the edges ⅛" inside the drawn line, then cut the silk and flannel together ½" outside the drawn line.

Second Application of Paint

Take the basted vest pieces outside and lay them on a plastic dropcloth, positioning the pieces in a row: side panel, armhole band, (exclude the band lining), center fronts, armhole band, side panel, center back.

Choose a sunny day to apply the overpainting: the paint will dry quickly, so that definite drops of color will form on the silk and not soak into the flannel. Colors for overpainting are diluted mixtures of Parma violet, yellow-green, and sienna, with black. (See Overpainting on page 19. Be sure to heat set after overpainting.) Begin at the shoulder edge of the vest center panels and make large drops, first purple, then sienna. Space the drops closely at the top edge, then widen the spacing and diminish the size of the drops towards the lower edge. Add yellow-green drops. Use the same overpaint colors to paint silk twill and silk ribbon. Alternate the purple and sienna along the ribbon to variegate the colors. Yellow-green ribbon will be used as stems for the flowers.

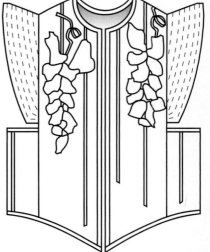

Position of appliqué and ribbon

Fabric Requirements
(for medium size)

- Light gray suèded silk: 1 yard
- Silk twill: purple, two full-width 2½" strips, burn thirty petal shapes
  sienna, two full-width 2½" strips, burn twenty-two petal shapes
  yellow-green full-width 3" strip, burn eight leaves
- Silk ribbon 3.8 mm: variegated purple-sienna 4 yards
  yellow-green 1 yard
- Phoenix pongee: purple 1 yard for lining
  multicolored ½ yard for bias binding
- Spun silk: variegated purple-sienna 1½" x 45" for bias binding
- Flannel: 1 yard

Additional Supplies

- Metallic pens: medium nib bronze and gold
- ¼"-wide white sable #6 flat brush with a tapered tip
- Pearlescent liquid acrylic ink: birdwing copper, moon violet
- Silver metallic thread

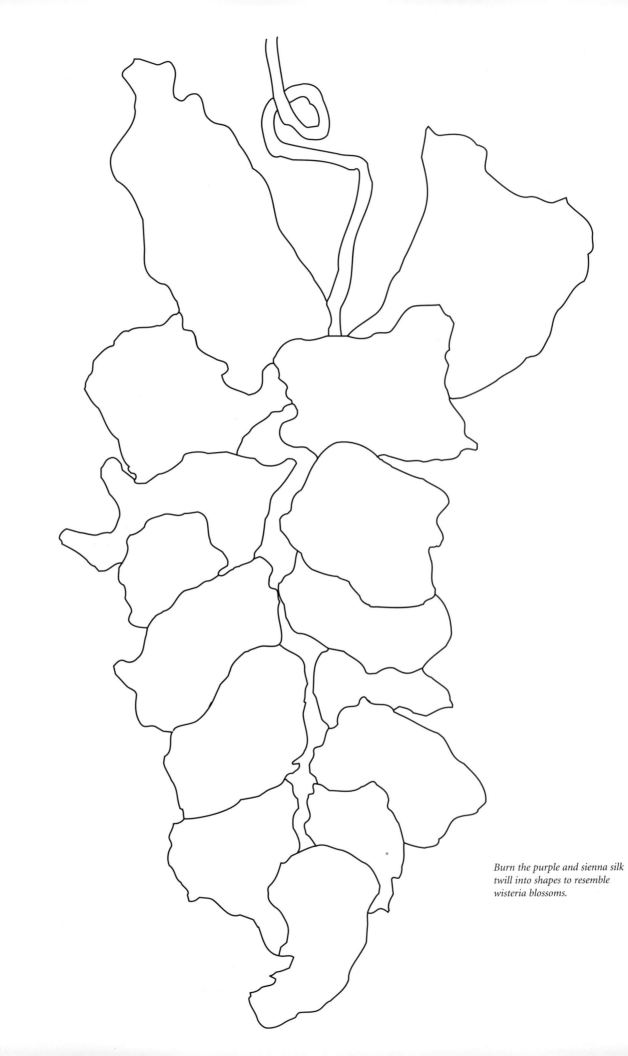

Burn the purple and sienna silk twill into shapes to resemble wisteria blossoms.

Preparing the Background

Begin the embellishment by stitching the purple and sienna silk ribbon on the side panels and on the center fronts and center back. Position the ribbons vertically with random spacing. Cut the ribbons in different lengths.

Burn the purple and sienna silk twill into shapes to resemble wisteria blossoms and the yellow green silk twill into leaf shapes. Pin clusters of wisteria petals on the center fronts and center back, on top of the ribbons. Add a few purple petals to the sienna cluster and a few sienna petals to the purple cluster. Pin the leaves at the top of the blossoms and add the yellow-green ribbon as a stem. Stitch the burned silk appliqué.

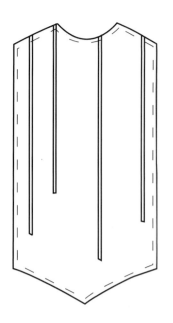

Top Stitching the Armhole Bands

Finish sewing the armhole bands according to the general directions. Top stitch the bands with a silver metallic sewing machine thread.

Test the method first on a scrap of fabric: it may be necessary to adjust the top tension on your sewing machine.

Metallic Pens and Ink

Before vest assembly, finish the final embellishment with metallic pens and ink. Lay all the pieces flat with the pattern pieces in a row as for the overpainting. Add curving lines of bronze and gold with metallic pens. Curve these around the wisteria and anywhere else that the design dictates, on the side panel and armhole bands. Add small amounts of Pearlescent liquid acrylic in copper and violet to accent the overpainting drops. Use the brush to apply the liquid acrylic. Highlight the wisteria petals by touching ink to the center of the petals. It is difficult to stitch through the fabric where metallic pens and inks have been applied, so apply these embellishments after all the hand stitching on the surface of the vest is done.

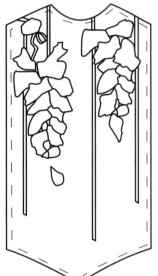

Assembling the Vest

See the General Directions on pages 46-47. The sample vest has a multicolored silk pongee as the binding on the neck and center front edges and side panels, and a purple and sienna spun silk binding to assemble the vest and on the lower edge.

Pleated Surface Vest with Appliqué

This vest pattern is very easy to make: it has only two pattern pieces, a V neckline, slightly curved lower front edge, generous armhole openings, and edges finished with a contrasting bias binding. A medium vest pattern is inserted in the back of this book, although any simple vest pattern that had two pieces would be suitable with this technique. The textured surface is accomplished by hand pleating painted spun silk fabric and heat setting the pleats. One and a half yards of silk is pleated to 30" length and the fabric is then bonded to a woven fusible interfacing to make a flat but manipulated vest surface. Cotton fabric could be used for the surface, but the pleats will not be as crisp as with lightweight silk. The pleated surface is decorated with appliqué, silk ribbon, sponge painting, and line drawing with metallic pens, ink, and paint.

Fabric Requirements

(for medium size)

- ◆ Spun silk: dark green 1½ yards
  gold ⅔ yard for lining
- ◆ Pongee: rose and gold, 6" strip of each for appliqué
  rose ⅔ yard for bias binding
- ◆ Rose silk 3.8 mm ribbon: 4 yards
- ◆ Woven fusible interfacing: 1¼ yards

Painting Supplies

- ¼"-wide white sable #6 flat brush with a tapered tip
- Metallic pens: silver and gold, very fine
- Pearlescent liquid acrylic ink: bell bronze and sundown magenta
- Gold metallic fabric paint or Liquitex iridescent gold
- Kitchen sponge: 1" x 1½"
- Net bag or nylon stocking: 3½" x 9"
- String: 1½ yards
- Clothespin to hang up the bundle

Pleating the Fabric

The pleated fabric requires a little extra time to prepare, because it must first be painted and heat set, pleated, then wet again and left to dry completely for one or two days so that the pleats will stay. Paint the spun silk fabric with an emerald and black mixture, using the Painting in a Pan or Basin technique on page 17. After the fabric has been heat set, lay the fabric flat on the work table with the selvages on the right and left and one torn edge of the fabric forward. Begin pleating the fabric with one hand on each selvage and gather up the fabric horizontally. The pleated fabric will be 36" wide and about 2" thick in each hand. Hold onto each end and twist in opposite directions until you form a roll that twists back on itself. Keep a firm grip on the ends and bring both ends together after the roll has twisted. Tie off the ends with a 1½ yard piece of string. Knot the string around both ends; wrap the remaining string down around the bundle and back up again, and tie it off at the top. Wet the wrapped bundle thoroughly and squeeze out the excess. Put the bundle in a net bag or old nylon stocking and tie off the open end with string. Place the bundle in the dryer with an old towel to cushion it. Dry hot until the bundle feels dry. This may take a while, and it may be easier after thirty minutes to remove the bundle and hang it up to dry. Leave it overnight and test the bundle the next day to see if the inside is dry. Remove the bundle from the bag and cut all the string. Carefully untwist the bundle, but do not open the pleats. Again hang this up to dry in the sun until the inside is completely dry. The pleats will not be crisp if the bundle is even slightly damp: it must be dry before you open the pleats.

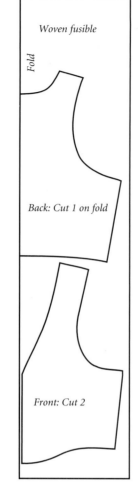

Woven fusible

Fold

Back: Cut 1 on fold

Front: Cut 2

Cutting Out the Vest Pattern

Use the vest pattern in the book, or a similar pattern. Cut the back on the fold and two fronts out of the woven fusible interfacing.

Preparing the Ironing Surface

Lay out several thicknesses of towels or a quilted pad on the work table. Pin the edges of the pleated silk, wrong side up, to the ironing surface. Open the pleats to 30" x 36". Lay the fusible interfacing, wrong side down, on the silk, the straight grain of the piece in line with the pleats.

The pleats will be vertical when the vest is worn. Iron the interfacing according to package directions to bond the pleated fabric to the interfacing, then cut out the pattern pieces.

Sewing On the Silk Ribbon

Draw a line 2½" to the left of the center back. Pin and stitch silk ribbon on this line, then space four more ribbons on the back piece and stitch. Repeat on center fronts. (See the ribbon spacing in the drawing on page 56.)

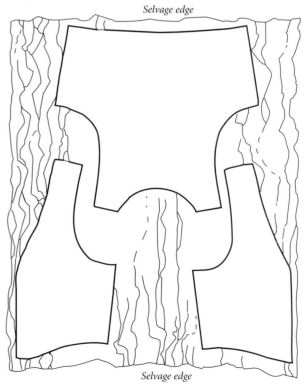

Selvage edge

Selvage edge

Appliqué

Draw patterns for templates for the leaves and flower petals. Trace the shapes on the silk pongee, cut them out allowing ¼" seam allowance, and clip the curves. Pin the appliqué shapes on the vest back and one front, and hand appliqué. Add stamens to the centers of the flowers by drawing with a very fine silver metallic pen.

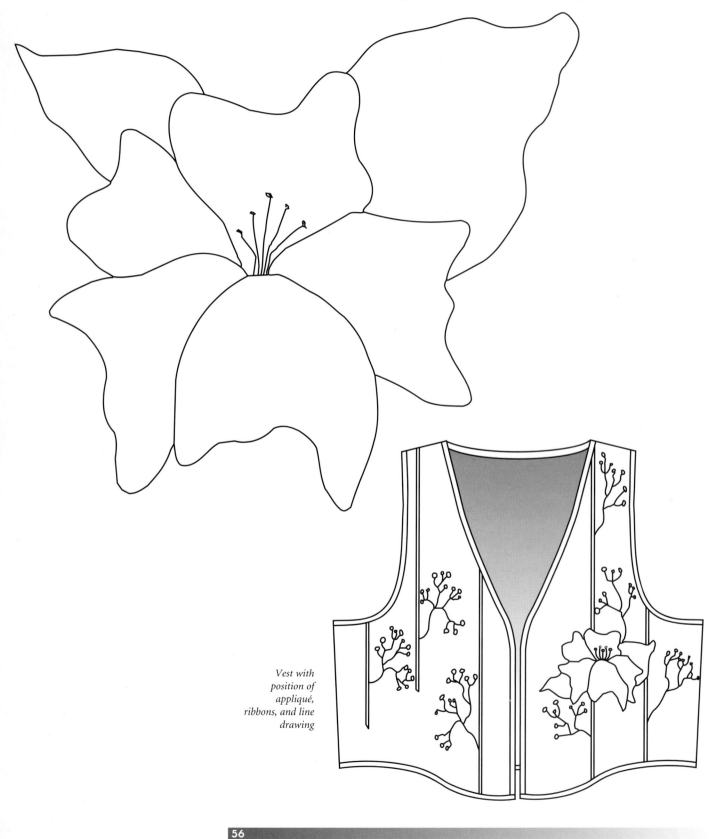

Vest with position of appliqué, ribbons, and line drawing

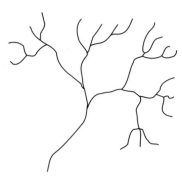

Line Drawing

Draw fine branch shapes on the vest with a silver pen. Begin the branches from the ribbon lines.

Add dots of sundown magenta Pearlescent liquid acrylic to the ends of the branches with the brush, and touch the top of the branch with the liquid acrylic to make the dot. Highlight a few of the dots by drawing circles with a gold pen around the dots.

Sponge Painting

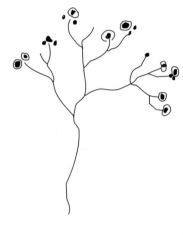

Use a tongue depressor to spoon 1 tablespoon of metallic gold textile paint or Liquitex iridescent gold into a pie pan. Moisten a 1" x 1½" sponge with water, and apply gold randomly across the vest surface, avoiding the branches and appliqué. Use the brush to stroke on small vertical lines of bell bronze Pearlescent liquid acrylic.

Cut Out and Sew the Lining

Cut out the gold spun silk lining and stitch the shoulder and side seams with ¼" seams. Press the seams open.

Assembling the Vest

Trim the pleated and embellished back and front to the same size as the paper pattern pieces. Sew the shoulder and side seams of the vest, and press the seams open. Pin the lining and the vest, wrong sides together, around the neck edge, lower edge, and armhole openings. Cut enough 1½"-wide rose bias binding to hem all the raw edges, beginning with the neck edge. Sew the binding on the lower edge and finish the two armhole openings. (See Seam Binding on page 27.)

Painting the Binding

After the vest is finished, decorate the binding with gold paint. Carefully sponge gold paint on the binding edges.

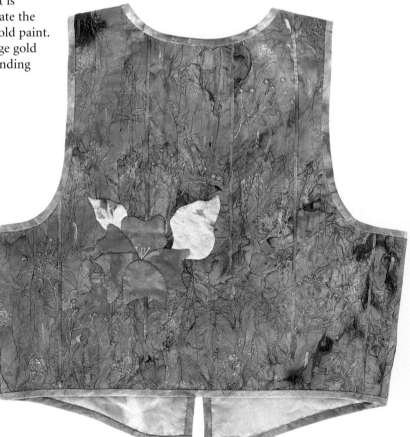

Gold Vest with Appliqué

The cap sleeve vest could be made in any color and any fabric, with appliqué in different shapes. A medium vest pattern is inserted at the back of the book. The medium size will fit a small, and it could be adjusted at the center front for a large. There are two pattern pieces, and it is loose-fitting. The sample vest is cut from one piece of gold pongee and embellished with silk ribbon, appliquéd Christmas ball ornaments, and wire-edged ribbon bows. A thin polyester batting is used for the foundation. The lining is gold muslin, and the cap sleeve and lower edges are finished with a muslin bias binding turned and stitched to the lining. The center front features loop buttonholes and fabric-covered buttons. Variegated wire-edged ribbon is used for the bows, or white wire-edged ribbon can be painted to complement the colors of the balls.

Fabric Requirements

(for medium size)

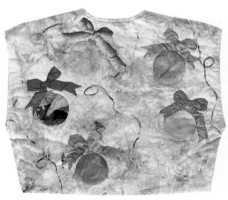

- ◆ Gold Phoenix pongee: 1 yard
- ◆ Gold muslin: 1 yard
- ◆ Batting: Thermore, 1 yard
- ◆ Silk twill: ⅛ yard each of periwinkle, mauve, purple, ultramarine, and sienna; cut two circles 3⅜" diameter from each color for Christmas balls.

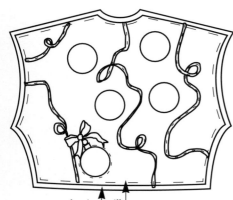

batting *silk*

Vest back
Baste two layers together.

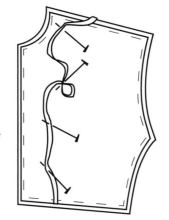

Vest front

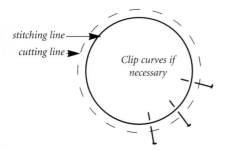

stitching line

cutting line

Clip curves if necessary

Small loop of silver sparkle yarn

Gray woven ribbon

Silk ball appliqué

Embellishments

- Wire-edged ribbon: ten pieces of 1" wide by 9" long, colors to accent the painted fabric
- Woven gray ribbon: ⅜" x 18"
- Silver Sparkle yarn: 18" heavy Kreinik Ombré™ #1000
- Gold silk 3.8 mm ribbon: 5 yards
- Gold metallic Kreinik Cord™ #002C sewing thread
- ⁹⁄₁₆" or similar size half-ball cover buttons: eight
- Very fine black or brown permanent marking pen
- Pattern tracing paper
- Template plastic 4" x 4"

Preparing the Background for Appliqué

Layer the batting and the gold silk, wrong sides together. Space the paper vest patterns 1" apart on the silk, and outline the pieces with a permanent marking pen. Carefully baste the silk to the batting by following ⅛" inside the drawn lines. Cut out pattern pieces ½" outside the drawn lines.

Making the Christmas Balls

Use the pattern to make a template for a 3⅜"-diameter circle for the Christmas balls. Draw two circles on each of the five silk twills with the permanent marking pen. Cut out circles, adding ¼" seam allowance. (See Hand Appliqué on page 25.)

Appliqué and Quilting

Beginning with the back of the vest, place five of the silk balls over the back.

Do not sew the balls in place yet. Arrange the gold silk ribbon in a random pattern around the balls. Pin the ribbon in place and remove the balls.

Stitch the ribbon in place, making sure the stitches go through the batting. Reposition the balls, pin around the edges, and hand appliqué through the batting.

Make a small loop of silver sparkle yarn for the hanger at top of each ball and pin in it place. Cut 1½" of the gray ribbon, and turn under seam allowance so the piece measures ⅝"; then stitch like a cap on the top of the ball.

Catch the sparkle yarn in the seam when you stitch the cap in place. Quilt through the silk and batting around each ball with gold metallic thread. After all the balls are in place, make the wire-edged ribbon bows and stitch them in place over the top hanger. Taper the ends of the bow, pull the wire out at least ½", and clip before stitching to the vest. Arrange the bows attractively so the sparkle yarn shows, and stitch the bows in place.

Repeat on the two front pattern pieces.

Pressing the Appliqué

Now gently steam iron the appliquéd pieces to flatten the wire-edged ribbon, and smooth out the silk if it has wrinkled. Be careful not to fold over the silk ribbon when you press.

Christmas ball appliqué pattern

Cutting Out the Lining

Cut out the lining at the same time you trim the pattern pieces to the correct size. (See Foundation Fabric and Lining on page 46.)

Assembling the Vest

Replace the standard foot on your sewing machine with a walking foot. Separate the vest pattern pieces and the lining pattern pieces. Right sides together, pin the vest back to the fronts at the shoulder and side seams, then stitch.

Repeat with the lining shoulder and side seams. Press open the seam allowance on the vest and lining.

Buttonhole Loops

Cut 1" bias strips from the gold pongee. Piece the bias if necessary to make 20" for loops. Fold the 1" bias strip in half, right sides together, to ½" wide and put a 25"-long piece of string inside the folded edge. Sew the top edge of the strip, catching the string in the seam. Sew with a ¼" seam allowance. Pull gently on the string to turn the bias right side out. Cut the top edge to remove the string. Press and cut into eight pieces, each 2½" long.

Pin the eight buttonhole loops to the right front edge of the center front, positioning them 2" from each loop center. A 2½" length of bias folded in half should be large enough to fit a ⁹⁄₁₆" covered button. If you use a smaller or larger button, adjust the size of the loop. Baste the loops in place.

Sewing the Lining to the Vest

Pin the right front lining, right sides together, to the right front silk vest edge, and stitch the right center front seam. This will catch the buttonhole loops in the seam. Repeat on the left front seam. While the vest is still wrong side out, pin the vest and lining around the neck opening, and stitch with a ¼" seam allowance. Clip the curved seam, turn the vest to the outside, and press sewn seams.

Top Stitching

Change the thread on top of the sewing machine to gold metallic thread and top stitch about ½" around the neck edge and the fronts. For best results, test a sample first, and loosen the top tension on the machine if necessary.

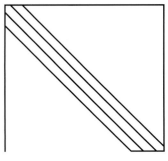

Cut bias strips 1" wide from gold pongee.

String

Sewing line

Fold

Continue for 20".

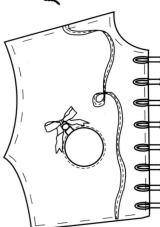

Pin button loops to right front edge, position 2" apart from center of each loop.

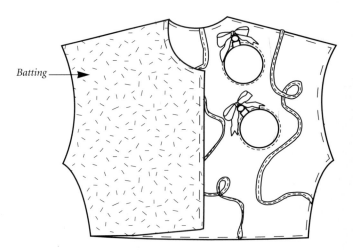

Batting

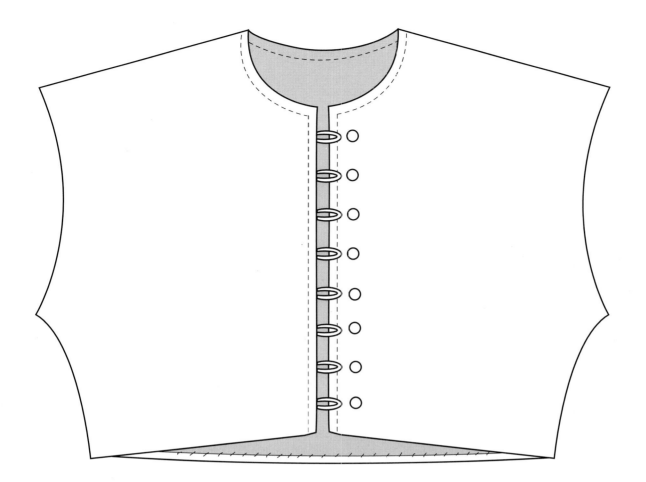

Finishing with Bias Binding Facings

Wrong sides together, pin along the armhole openings and the bottom edge, matching up the side and shoulder seams. Cut a 1½"-wide bias strip from the remaining painted muslin lining fabric. Cut enough bias to go around the armhole openings and the bottom edge. Piece the bias if the strips are not long enough. Sew bias binding to armhole edges, with right sides together. Fold the beginning edge of the bias strip ½". Pin the bias folded edge at the underarm seam line and stitch the armhole edge, overlapping the bias binding at the starting point. Clip any curves, and press the bias binding and the seam allowance to the lining. Turn under raw edge of binding and slipstitch the folded edge of the binding to the inside lining. Sew bias binding to the bottom edge, extending ½" beyond center fronts. Then turn under the bias raw edge seam allowance. Be sure that both right and left center fronts measure the same length. You can adjust the center front length when turning the bias binding on the bottom edge to the inside. Fold in the raw ends of the binding, and slipstitch the folded edge of the binding to the inside lining.

Covered Buttons

Cut circles from silk to cover the eight ⁹⁄₁₆" half-ball cover buttons, according to the package directions, and cover the buttons. I matched the button fabric to the appliquéd balls; you could also match the buttons to the vest color. Position buttons to line up with loops, and sew the buttons in place.

Chapter Six

Cloth Dolls

Honey, Sweetie, Lyla, and Brenda can be made with plain cotton muslin for the basic shapes, hand-painted cottons, or commercial fabrics. The dolls have silk roses, ribbons, and seed bead decorations. When I make a doll, I begin with the fabric choice and determine the embellishments as the doll develops a personality. There are two samples here from each doll pattern, to illustrate how the basic doll can be changed by the fabric choices and trims.

General Directions For Dolls

Measurements for fabrics include the front and back of each pattern. Fold the fabric for each pattern piece in half, right sides together, and trace the patterns on the wrong side with a pencil. Stitch along the drawn lines, leaving the seam open where indicated for stuffing. Cut out the pieces ¼" from the stitched line. Clip the curves to the stitching line.

Turning and Stuffing Tool

My choice is to use a hemostat for turning the pattern pieces right side out and for stuffing. This implement is available at some hobby and craft stores, or you can call the supplier listed in the Resource Guide for a store in your area. You can use any other convenient tool to turn and stuff the doll.

Turn the pattern pieces right side out and run the hemostat tip along the seam on the inside to smooth the seam. Stuff each piece and slipstitch the opening, or attach the piece to another piece where indicated.

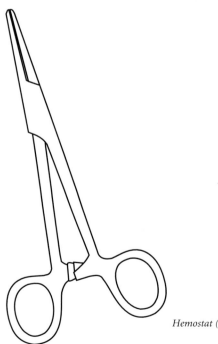

Hemostat (not actual size)

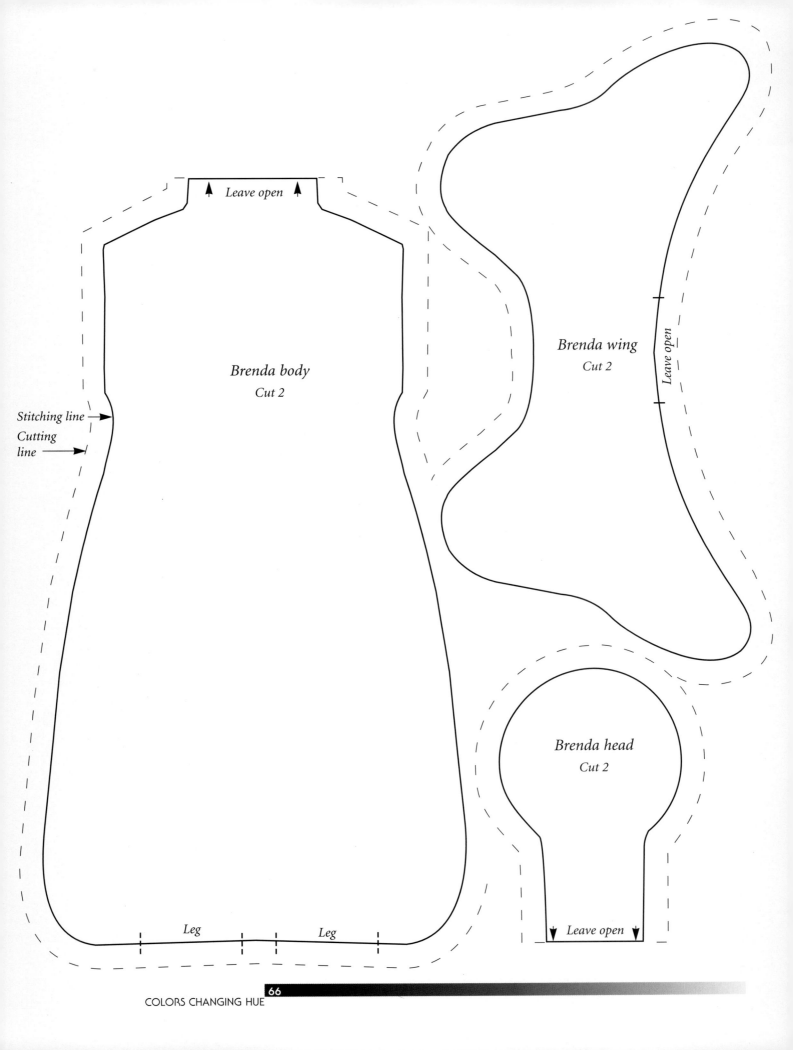

Leave open

Stitching line

Cutting
line

Brenda body
Cut 2

Leg   Leg

Brenda wing
Cut 2

Leave open

Brenda head
Cut 2

Leave open

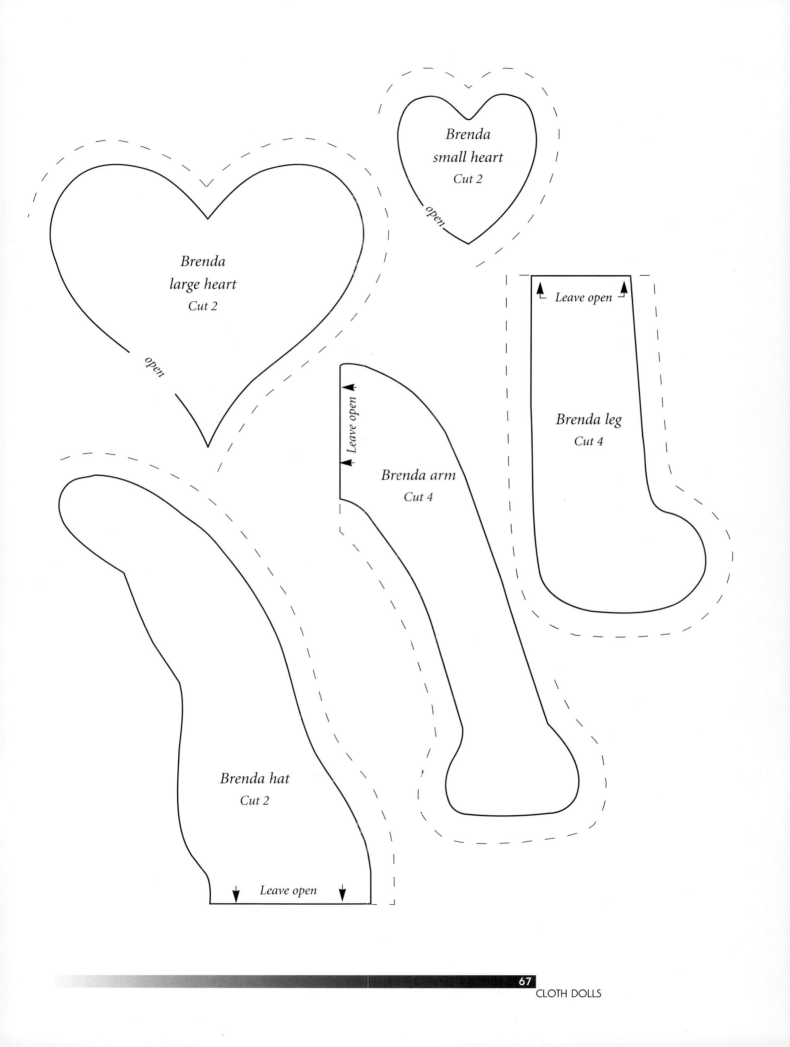

Brenda
small heart
Cut 2

open

Brenda
large heart
Cut 2

open

Leave open

Brenda leg
Cut 4

Leave open

Brenda arm
Cut 4

Brenda hat
Cut 2

Leave open

Brenda

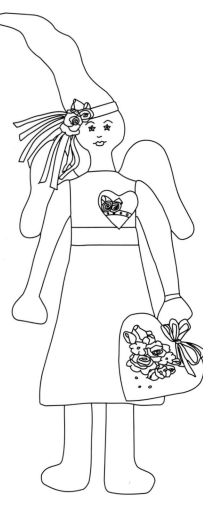

Two sample dolls are shown, and the specific directions are for the pastel doll. Brenda has a shaped pattern piece cut from painted fabric to form her dress. The head is sewn into the neck seam, the arms are sewn to the shoulder edge of the dress, and the legs are included in the bottom seam. The hat is stuffed and sewn to the head, and wings are stitched to the back of the doll. Two stuffed hearts decorate this doll: the large one is attached to the wrist and the small one is pinned to the bodice. The small heart could be placed elsewhere. (You might also want to remove and wear it.) The project directions are for muslin painted gold, blue, and green for the doll and the large heart, for silk painted gray for the wings, and mauve for the small heart. The silk roses for trim are available by mail order or can be made from silk fabric or ribbon. (See Ribbons and Roses on page 14.)

Fabric Requirements

- ◆ Muslin: gold and blue-green doll body 5" x 20"
  gold legs 6" x 7"
  gold head and arms 3" x 21"
  gold hat 5½" x 6"
  blue heart 3¾" x 7"
- ◆ Silk twill: gray wings 3¾" x 14"
- ◆ Phoenix pongee: mauve heart 2½" x 4½"
  gold waistband 1¼" x 7"
  gold headband and wing band 1" x 25" bias strip
- ◆ Stuffing: Poly-fil (about ⅓ of a 12 oz. bag)

Embellishments

- ◆ Silk roses: twelve in assorted colors and sizes
- ◆ Silk 3.8 mm ribbon: purple 2 yards, gold 1 yard
- ◆ Gold seed beads: sixteen
- ◆ Small star sequins: two
- ◆ Tulip® paint: pink
- ◆ Very fine permanent marking pens: red and brown
- ◆ Small gold safety pin
- ◆ Liquitex iridescent gold
- ◆ Kitchen sponge 1" x 1"
- ◆ White craft glue

Doll Construction

Body

Fold the 5" x 20" fabric in half right sides together to 5" x 10". Trace the pattern onto the fabric and pin along the drawn line.

Legs

Fold the 6" x 7" fabric in half, right sides together, to 3½" x 6". Trace two legs, stitch, clip curves, and turn. Stuff to ½" of the top edge. Pin the legs, right sides together, at the bottom edge of the body where indicated. The legs will be sewn into this edge when the body is sewn together.

Stitch around the body, catching the legs in the seam and leaving the neck open. Turn the body right side out and use the hemostat to pull the legs one at a time through the neck opening. Stuff the body.

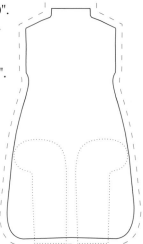

Head and Arms

Fold the 3" x 21" fabric in half, right sides together, and trace the head and two arms. Stitch the head and arms (leaving an opening as indicated on the pattern), clip curves, turn, and stuff. Turn in ¼" seam allowance on the shoulder edge of the arms. Pin the head into the neck opening and slipstitch the head to the opening. Pin the arms to the body at the top of the shoulder, matching the top seam of the arm and the body. Slipstitch the arms to the body.

Hat

Fold the 5½" x 6" fabric right sides together, to 2¾" x 6" and trace the hat. Stitch, clip curves, turn, and stuff. Turn under ¼" seam allowance on the lower edge of the hat and slipstitch the hat to the head.

Headband and Wing Band

Fold the 1" x 25" strip in half, right sides together, trim the ends, and stitch across one end and side with ¼" seam on a machine; use the string method as described for the Gold Vest with Appliqué. (See Buttonhole Loops on page 62.) Turn right side out. Trim the ends and cut it into two 12" pieces. Hand hem the ends. Wrap one band around the junction of the hat and head, leaving 3½" of each end hanging at the left side of the head. Stitch to secure.

Wing

Fold the 3¾" x 14" strip to 3¾" x 7". Trace the wing, stitch, clip curves, turn, and stuff. Slipstitch the open seam. Mark 6" on the wing band and pin the band to the back of the body ½" below the neck edge. Stitch the band across the 6" center mark and down on both sides for 1". Lay the wing over the band and fold down the top 6" of the band. Stitch the band together under the wing, and slipstitch around the band and into the wing to secure the band to the top of the wing.

Waistband

On a pressing surface, lay the 1¼" x 7" fabric right side down, then fold in the raw edges to make a ½" x 7" band, and press. Wrap the band around the waist, overlapping in the back; fold in the raw edge and slipstitch.

Face

Decorate the head band with three silk roses and silk ribbon. Draw eyebrows and the nose curve with a brown pen, and draw lips with a red pen. Glue two star sequins with two gold seed beads for eyes and fill in the lips with pink paint.

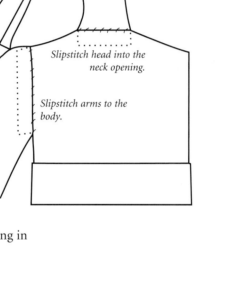

Headband
Slipstitch hat to head.

Slipstitch head into the neck opening.

Slipstitch arms to the body.

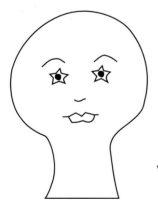

Large Heart

Fold the 3¾" x 7' piece, right sides together, to 3¾" x 3½". Trace the heart, stitch, clip curves, and stuff. Slipstitch the side opening. Decorate the heart with seven silk roses. Sew eight gold seed beads around the roses. Cut 24" of purple silk ribbon and make a small bow, with one loop long enough to fit over the wrist. Tack the ribbon at the center top of the heart. Put the large ribbon loop over the wrist and stitch to secure it.

wing

wing band

Slip-stitch waist-band in back.

Small Heart

Fold the 2½" x 4½" piece, right sides together, to 2½" x 2¼". Trace, stitch, clip curves, and stuff the heart. Slipstitch the side opening. Decorate the heart with a piece of silk ribbon, six gold seed beads, and two silk roses. Sew the small gold safety pin on the back of the heart. Pin the heart onto the bodice.

Sponge Painting

Put a small amount of iridescent gold into a pie pan. Moisten the sponge with water and squeeze out the excess. Sponge gold paint onto the hat and skirt.

Honey

The choice of fabric and decorations gives this doll character. Painted muslin or cotton fabrics are suitable. The samples are made from painted orange muslin and glazed cotton chintz. The orange doll is decorated with sequins, seed beads, and silk ribbons.

Fabric Requirements

◆ Orange muslin: body 2¾" x 7" folded to 2¾" x 3½"
  legs 2½" x 6" (cut two)
  arms 2" x 4" (cut two)
  head 2" x 5" folded to 2" x 2½"

Embellishments

◆ Red silk 3.8 mm ribbon: 1½ yards
◆ Thirty red seed beads
◆ Three red heart sequins
◆ Three red star sequins
◆ Two large red rhinestones
◆ Small red heart button

Sewing the Doll

Follow the General Directions on page 65 to prepare the pattern pieces.

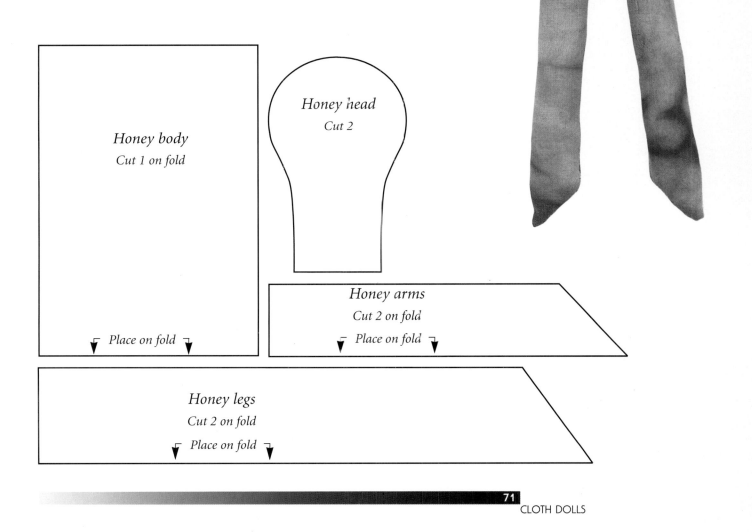

Honey body
Cut 1 on fold

Place on fold

Honey head
Cut 2

Honey arms
Cut 2 on fold

Place on fold

Honey legs
Cut 2 on fold

Place on fold

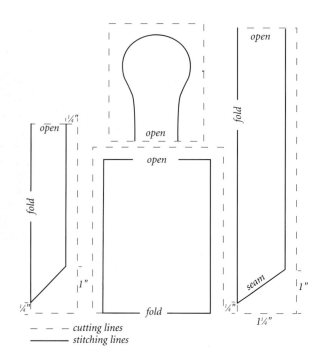

--- cutting lines
—— stitching lines

Stuffing the Doll

The arms and legs are of small diameter, so you may need a smaller tool for stuffing. First turn under the seam allowance at the top edge of the arms and legs, and finger press. Avoid lumps in the arms and legs when stuffing. Place the stuffed arms and legs on the table and, with the flat palm of your hand, roll the arms and legs to smooth out the stuffing.

Assembling the Doll

Pin the head into the neck opening and slipstitch it. Pin the open end of the arms over the corners of the shoulders and slipstitch. Sew the legs to the body, with the corners of the body extending over the legs.

Decorating the Doll

Stitch sequins and seed beads to the body. Finish the neck with a silk ribbon bow. Cut the ribbon into three 12" and two 8" lengths, layer the ribbons, and tie them around the neck. Stitch through the bow to secure it.

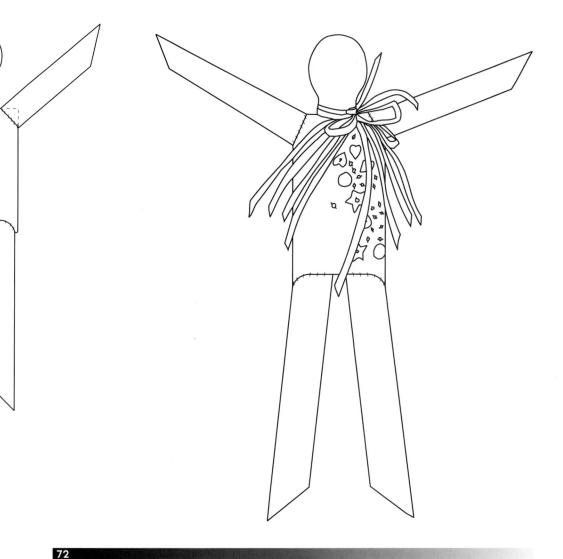

Sweetie

This doll has a muslin body decorated by wrapping silk fabric around it, then stitching with seed beads to cover the stitches and to secure the wrapping. This small doll is a perfect size to use as a Christmas tree ornament. Any color of fabric can be used: the sample is gold with purple trim.

Fabric Requirements

- Gold muslin: body 2½" x 6" folded to 2½" x 3"
  legs 1½" x 3½" (cut two)
  arms 1½" x 2¾" (cut two)
  head 1¾" x 4" folded to 1¾" x 2"
- Gold silk twill: 3" x 6" (cut two)
  6" x 6" square folded on the bias and cut into two triangles (burn edges)

Embellishments

- Purple silk 3.8 mm ribbon: 16"
- Silk roses: four
- Seventy-five gold seed beads
- Gesso (an artist material made from glue and white chalk, used as an underpainting medium)
- Cardinal red paint: two drops
- Very fine permanent pens: black and red
- White craft glue
- Gold medium nib metallic pen

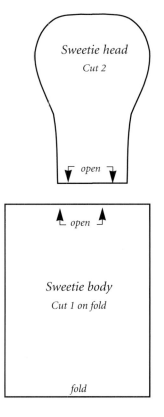

Sweetie head
Cut 2

open

Sweetie arms
Cut 2 on fold

fold

open

Sweetie legs
Cut 2 on fold

fold

open

open

Sweetie body
Cut 1 on fold

fold

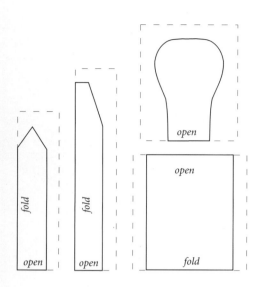

Draw the face.

Sewing the Doll

Follow the General Directions on page 65.

Assembling the Doll

Pin the head into the center of the top edge of the body, and slipstitch the whole seam from corner to corner. Pin the open end of the arms over the corners of the shoulders and slipstitch. Sew the legs to the body, with the corners of the body extending over the legs.

Painting the Head

Mix ½ teaspoon of gesso with 2 drops of red paint, and mix well. Paint the front and back of the head and let it dry. Draw curly lines on the top and back of the head with the gold metallic pen to simulate hair. Draw the face. Fill in the mouth with the red pen. Add two gold dots to the cheeks.

Decorating with Silk and Beads

Begin with the two 3" x 6" strips of silk twill and burn the edges or press raw edges under. (See Burning Silk on page 26.) Starting at the toe on the right side, wrap and pin the strip up the leg and across the body. Repeat with the other strip on the left leg. Pin the point of the silk triangle at the right wrist, and wrap it around the arm and across the body. Repeat with the other triangle on the left arm. You may have to adjust the silk wrapping and the pins to make the fabric cover the doll.

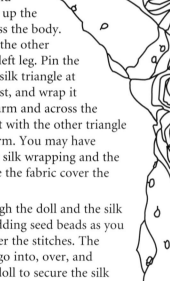

Sew through the doll and the silk wrapping, adding seed beads as you stitch to cover the stitches. The stitches can go into, over, and around the doll to secure the silk firmly and shape the wrapping to the body and legs.

Finishing

Add silk roses to the bodice. Make a purple silk ribbon bow and glue it to the forehead; glue a silk rose to the center of the ribbon.

Lyla

Lyla is a large doll with shaped legs and arms. She is constructed like Honey and Sweetie. There are two samples of Lyla, each with a special feature which could be used to decorate other dolls. Lilac Lyla has an iron-on face, burned silk wrappings around a muslin body, and a wire-edged ribbon hat. Lyla-san has a painted face and a multicolored fabric body trimmed with silk ribbon and roses. The hat on Lyla-san was made by experimenting with twisting and wrapping raveled threads. I collected all of the raveled threads from previously torn strips of silk and used them to make a head ornament.

◆ Directions for Lilac Lyla

Lilac Lyla has a plain unbleached muslin body sprayed with gold paint after she was stuffed and assembled. The breast plate is a piece of iridescent plastic, and the body embellishment is burned silk with gold seed beads covering the stitches. The face was drawn on a separate piece of fabric ironed onto Wonder-Under™, then heat set onto the head. Sequins are glued on to cover the raw edge of the face. The hat is made from painted wire-edged ribbon and decorated with silk ribbon and burned silk.

Fabric Requirements

- Muslin: ¼ yard
- Purple silk twill: 4" x 15"
- Rust silk organza sheer: 3" by 12"
- Wonder-Under: 4" x 4"

Embellishments

- Sixty-five gold seed beads
- Beige silk 3.8 mm ribbon: 1 yard
- Iridescent plastic or similar product: 3" x 4"
- Variegated purple wire-edged ribbon: 3" x 12"
- Gold sequin trim: 5"
- Liquitex iridescent gold
- Very fine permanent pens: black, red, and brown
- FabriColor or FabricMate pens: purple and gold
- White craft glue

Basic Doll Construction

Trace the doll pattern onto the wrong side of the body fabric. Stitch all the pattern pieces except the arms, clip the corners, turn, and stuff. Fold in ¼" seam allowance at the neck opening, and pin the head in the center of the opening. Slipstitch the head to the body at the neck edge.

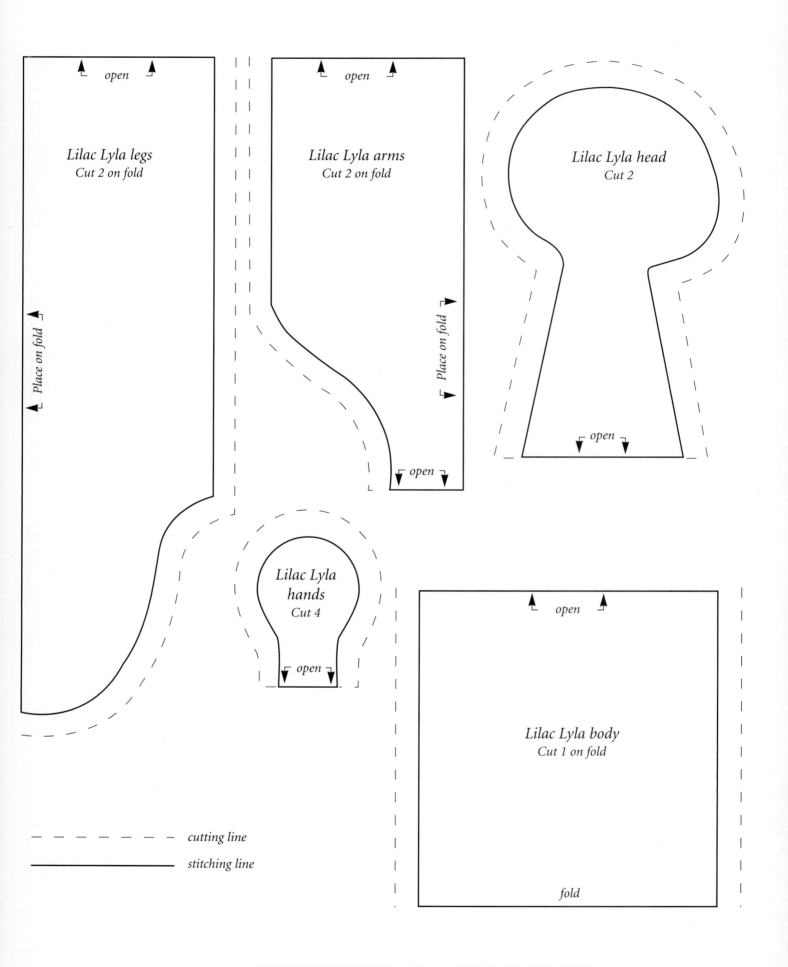

Lilac Lyla legs
Cut 2 on fold

open

Place on fold

Lilac Lyla arms
Cut 2 on fold

open

Place on fold

open

Lilac Lyla head
Cut 2

open

Lilac Lyla
hands
Cut 4

open

Lilac Lyla body
Cut 1 on fold

open

fold

cutting line

stitching line

Sewing on the Arms

Sew the curved seams of the arms. Stuff the hands, fold in ¼" seam allowance at the wrist edge of the arm, and pin the hand in the opening. Slipstitch the hand in the opening at the wrist edge, then finish stuffing the arms to ¼" of the top edge. Fold in ¼" seam allowance at the shoulder, pin to the body, and hand stitch the arms to the body.

Sewing the Legs to the Body

Position the legs with the curved edges (heels) together. Fold in ¼" seam allowance at the top edge of the legs, pin the legs in place at the lower edge of the body, and slipstitch in place.

Drawing the Face

Following product directions, heat set Wonder-Under to the wrong side of a 4" x 4" piece of muslin. Trace the oval face pattern on the muslin and cut out. Draw the eyes, nose, and mouth with brown and red pens.

Use the remainder of the prepared muslin to re-draw the face features if necessary. Heat set the face on the doll head, according to the product directions. Add color to the lips and eyebrows with the fabric pens.

Decorating the Doll

To cover the raw edge of the applied face, glue a piece of sequin trim around the edge. Decorate the center front of the body with a piece of iridescent plastic for the breast plate. This plastic is pliable and it can be secured with stitches to the doll body. The rest of the doll is decorated with burned silk. Follow the general directions for burned silk embellishment for Sweetie on page 74 to decorate the body. This method requires wrapping the burned silk around the doll and re-adjusting the pieces until it looks like clothing.

Gather the wire-edged ribbon to make a circle for the hat; stitch to secure the circle. Add bits of burned silk to the underside of the hat, and a silk ribbon bow. Glue the hat onto the head and add more burned silk and ribbon to the back of the hat.

Lilac Lyla

◆ Directions for Lyla-San

The body of Lyla-san is made from painted cotton duck. The face is drawn on the muslin head prepared with a white gesso background. The body is embellished with silk roses and ribbons, and ravel threads from torn silk are used to decorate the hat. Lyla-san has an alternate sleeve pattern. The legs are cut the same as Lilac Lyla but sewn onto the body in a different position, with the shaped edge to the back of the doll.

Fabric Requirements

- ◆ Multicolored cotton duck: ¼ yard
- ◆ Muslin: 4" x 6"
- ◆ Silk charmeuse: 1¾" by 26" sewn into a ⅝" tube, then cut into a 20" and a 6" piece

Embellishments

- ◆ Silk 3.8 mm ribbon: 24" each moss green, olive, and orange
- ◆ Silk roses: five clusters of roses and five single roses
- ◆ Chinese coin
- ◆ Raveled silk threads from previous projects
- ◆ Gesso: two teaspoons
- ◆ Very fine permanent marking pen: black
- ◆ FabricMate or FabriColor pens: green, pink, and lavender
- ◆ Gold medium nib metallic pen
- ◆ White craft glue

Basic Doll Construction

Trace the doll pattern body, two arms, and two legs onto the wrong side of the painted cotton duck. Trace the doll head and two hands on the wrong side of the doubled muslin. Stitch all the pattern pieces except the hands and arms, clip the corners, turn, and stuff. Slipstitch the head to the body at the neck edge.

Sewing on the Hands

First stuff the hands to ½" of the opening, then pin the hands at the wrist edge, right sides together. Machine stitch the hands in the wrist edge of the arm pattern piece and continue stitching the underarm seams. Turn right sides out. Stuff the arms and hand stitch the arms to the body. (See page 81.)

Sewing the Legs to the Body

Lyla-san has the curved edges (heels) turned to the back. Position the legs at the lower edge of the body. Fold in ¼" seam allowance at the top edge of the legs and pin in place, then slipstitch the legs to the body.

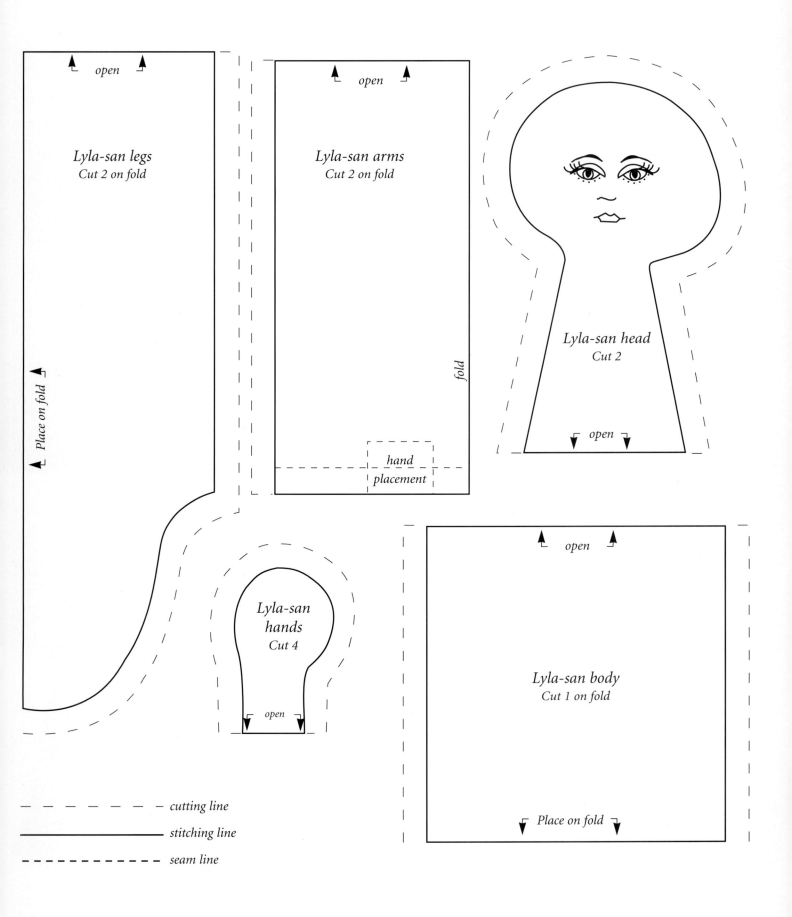

open

Lyla-san legs
Cut 2 on fold

Place on fold

open

Lyla-san arms
Cut 2 on fold

fold

hand
placement

Lyla-san head
Cut 2

open

Lyla-san
hands
Cut 4

open

Lyla-san body
Cut 1 on fold

open

Place on fold

— — — — — cutting line

——————— stitching line

- - - - - - - - - - seam line

Painting the Face

Paint gesso on the front and back of the head. (See the directions for Sweetie on page 74.) Draw curly hair with the gold pen over the back of the head and around the front. Draw the eyes, nose, and mouth with the black pen. Color in the eye shadow, lips, and cheeks with fabric pens.

wrist edge

Sewing the legs to the body

Decorating the Doll

Since the body of Lyla-san is made from a multicolored fabric, the decorations should complement the colors. A 20" silk charmeuse tube makes a neck band, decorated with silk ribbon and roses. Hem both edges of the ⅝" charmeuse tube by hand. Glue or stitch this in place and fasten a Chinese coin on a silk ribbon around the neck. Sew silk ribbons over the tube from the shoulder to the top of the legs, and add silk ribbon streamers. (See photo on page 79.) The hat is a combination of a 6" tube of silk charmeuse, raveled silk threads, silk ribbon, burned silk, and silk roses. I wrapped the tube around the head and added the other materials. This calls for experimentation with creative stitching and gluing to make a decorative ornament.

Chapter Seven

Gifts & Wrapping

I have encouraged you to experiment with colors when painting fabric and to use excess paint on extra fabrics. Some of this bonus fabric can be used in the preceding projects as small color accents. Often, you will have a generous amount of fabric that does not find a place in a specific project. I always find a use for painted fabric, and here are some gift projects which can be made with the extras. I also like to make the gift presentation unique, so I will share methods of making gift wrappings. I will give you some basic ideas, but some of the embellishments can be done in your own style. For instance, I have made a Harvest Heart framed picture using burned silk appliqué. It is much easier for me to burn the edges of the silk than to turn them under like traditional appliqué. The Harvest Heart could be done with traditional appliqué or crazy quilting or silk ribbon embroidery if you prefer. The shapes and presentations are my suggestions, but be free with your personal style.

Collage Heart

This project is very simple, but when it is framed it becomes a unique gift. Small bits of leftover silk twill are burned to make small petals. The silk is then mounted with a glue stick onto a colored mat board, available at an art supply store. My local store has a good color selection of pre-cut mat board, sold by size, the remainders from larger mats.

Fabric Requirements

- Silk twill: 1" and ¾" strips. Cut them into squares and burn the following: seven green leaves; six salmon petals; seven lavender petals; four orange circles; seven light blue petals; three dark red petals cut to ⅜"; one dark red ¾" circle; seven gold petals; five periwinkle petals.

Materials

- UHU® stic glue stick 1"
- Very fine metallic pens: gold and silver
- Dark tan mat board: 8" x 10"
- Heart template (page 84, dashed line)

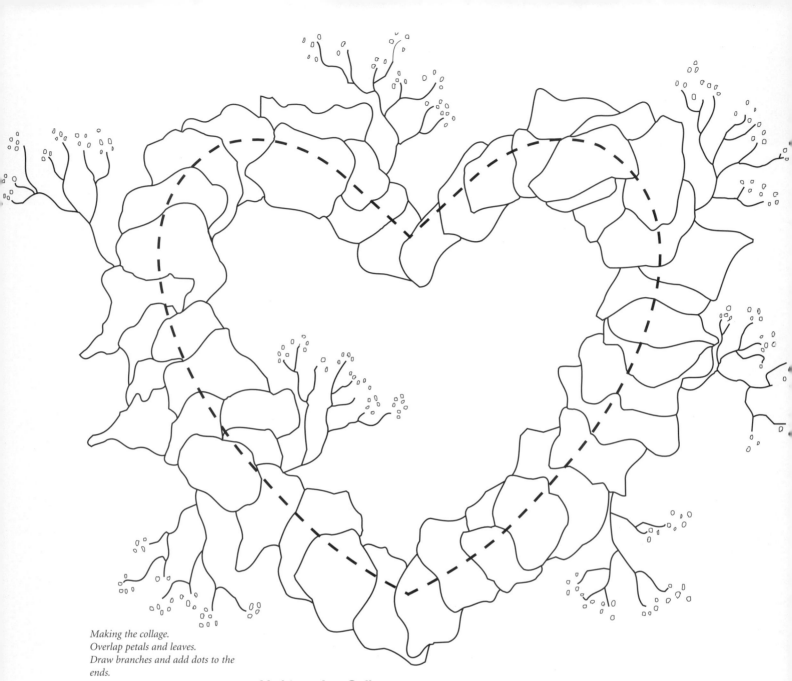

Making the collage.
Overlap petals and leaves.
Draw branches and add dots to the
ends.

Making the Collage

Center the template on the mat and trace the heart onto the mat with a gold pen. This will serve as a guideline for placement of the flowers and leaves and will not show in the finished project. Position the leaves and petals by overlapping the shapes around the heart. Be careful to balance the color and design.

Be sure to keep a heart shape in the center as well as on the outside when you arrange the petals. Carefully move the shapes, and glue each in place.

Drawing the Branches

Use the gold pen to draw branches showing from behind the petals. Add silver dots to the ends of the branches.

Finding a Frame

The sample collage was framed in a gold-tone ready-made frame from my local art supply store. Be sure to clean the glass on both sides before mounting your collage. You can decorate the frame yourself if you can't find one to match your collage. Liquitex Interference and Iridescent Gold can be sponged on to decorate a plain frame.

Harvest Heart

I used gold silk charmeuse to make a heart and decorated it with burned silk flowers. This makes a very impressive gift: I usually have it professionally placed in a shadow-box frame. A full-sized pattern is in the back of the book.

Fabric Requirements

- ◆ Flannel: 15" square
- ◆ Gold silk charmeuse: 15" square
- ◆ Gold muslin: 15" square
- ◆ Silk twill: personal choice of colors and flower and leaf shapes
- ◆ Heart pattern

Embellishments

- ◆ Metallic pens: gold and silver
- ◆ Liquitex Interference: gold
- ◆ Metallic sewing thread: gold

Making the Heart

I used a three-layer construction by putting flannel down first, with silk charmeuse right side up over it. The third layer is muslin, placed right sides together over the silk. Pin all three layers together and trace the 13" heart template on the muslin.

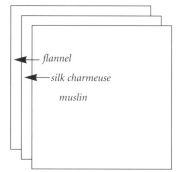

flannel
silk charmeuse
muslin

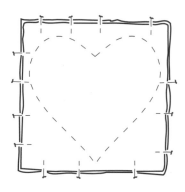

Stitch on the drawn line and cut out the heart ¼" from the stitching line; clip the curves. Make a 2" cut in only the muslin layer in the center back. Turn the silk and flannel layers together through this slit and press.

Top Stitching the Edge

Change the presser foot to a walking foot on the sewing machine. Use gold thread and top stitch ⅜" around the edge of the heart. Slipstitch the muslin to close the back opening.

Burning the Flowers

Re-read the directions for the Summer Bouquet Silk Quilt on page 36. Follow the directions for burned silk flowers. In this project you can arrange the flowers and leaves on the heart and use colors of your choice. You can also use traditional appliqué or any other stitchery technique. Stitch your flowers and leaves in place. In the photo on page 85 you can see how I designed my Harvest Heart.

Painting the Heart

You can add gold branches to the appliqué if you like with a gold metallic pen. You can sponge gold Interference on the unembellished parts of the heart to add a light sparkle, and add small dots of Pearlescent ink to highlight the branches.

Finding a Frame

Since the heart is not stiff enough to hang by itself, it needs a frame or background board. Because it is almost square, you may want to have it professionally mounted and framed. For this sample, I gave the framer white silk to cover the mounting board. You might also tack the finished heart to colored mat board with long stitches.

Approximate position of flowers and leaves on the heart (not to scale)

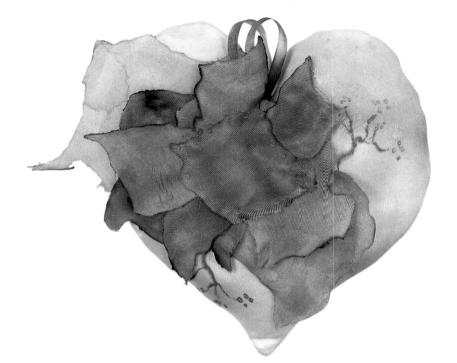

Stuffed Heart

This is a somewhat smaller version of the Harvest Heart, stuffed with Poly-fil. I usually use a single burned silk flower to decorate this 4½" heart. It can be used to decorate a gift or as a tree ornament, or you could put scented potpourri in the heart for a sachet.

Fabric Requirements

- Gold silk charmeuse: 6" x 12"
- Flannel: 6" x 12"
- Poly-fil
- Silk twill: personal choice of flower color and leaf shapes
- Heart pattern

Embellishments

- Metallic pens: gold and silver
- Silk 3.8 mm ribbon: 14"
- White craft glue

Making the Heart

Layer the silk charmeuse over the flannel, wrong sides together. Fold the two layers to make a 6" x 6" square. Trace the template on the flannel and stitch around the edge.

Stuffed heart pattern

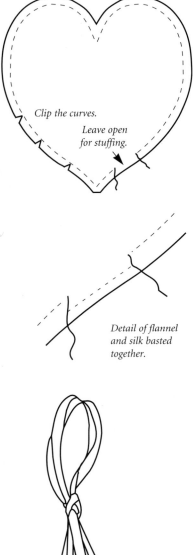

Clip the curves.

Leave open for stuffing.

Leave the seam open ¾"; cut out the heart ¼" from stitching line, and baste layers of flannel and silk together at the opening edge before stuffing.

Clip the curves, turn right side out, and stuff. Slipstitch the opening after stuffing.

Decorating the Heart

Make a burned silk flower and leaves in your choice of colors. Overlap the leaves and petal shapes. Stitch to secure. I stitched only around the center petal which overlapped the other shapes. The remaining petal and leaf edges stay free.

Fold the silk ribbon in half twice to make a knotted double loop. Snip the bottom loop. Glue the knot to the back of the heart in the top center, so the heart can hang from the loop. Draw branches with the metallic pens.

Detail of flannel and silk basted together.

Folded ribbon for heart

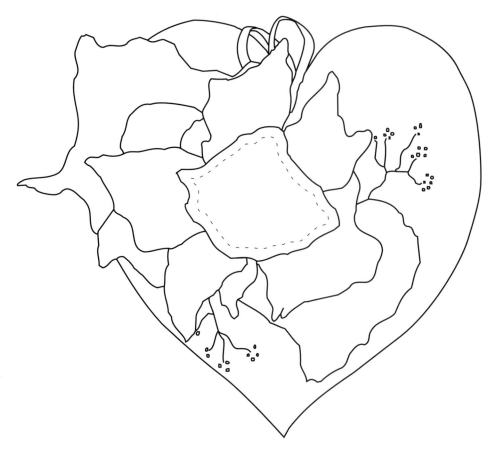

COLORS CHANGING HUE

Wrapping

Often when I make a gift it is difficult to find an appropriate box and wrapping; it is easier to make my own. In the photo you will see a variety of wrapping styles. All the fabrics were leftover painted fabrics except for two, made specifically for these packages. The gold and blue packages (left) are wrapped with a silk scarf and a man's cotton handkerchief. White silk scarves with a rolled hem are available from suppliers listed in the Resource Guide. These make great gifts by themselves, but I also use them to wrap books or other gifts. Men's 16" square 100% cotton handkerchiefs are available in packages of 6 or 12. The handkerchiefs also have a rolled hem and make wonderful wrappings for paperback books or small packages.

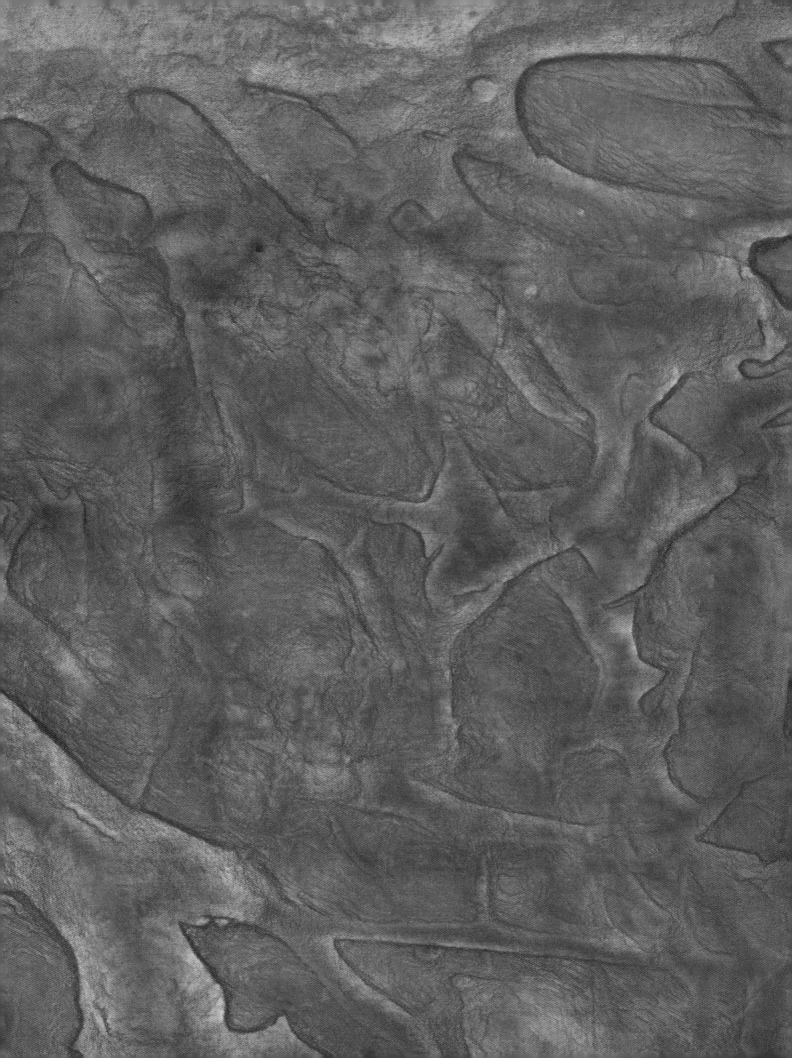

Painting the Edges

When you use a piece of fabric to wrap a package, it is important to finish the raw edges to make the wrapping attractive and to prevent raveling. This is why pre-hemmed scarves and handkerchiefs are convenient. If you have a serger or rolled hem attachment for your machine, you can finish the edges easily and quickly by machine.

Another method for finishing the edges is to paint Liquitex iridescent gold or copper along the raw edges. In the photo, notice the gold paint on the purple tie and the square wrapping in the middle. Lay the fabric on plastic and, with a flat #4 artist's brush, apply metallic paint ½" along the edges. It will dry quickly and you can then carefully cut cleanly through the painted edges with scissors. I usually try to make the pretty painted edge show: place the item in the center of the wrapping and fold the four corners in. You may have to try this several times to get it right.

Bags

Another great wrapping, and one of my personal favorites, is a bag. I cut the fabric to fit, with spare room for the contents. I make the bag as simple as possible, constructed like a pillowcase. I make a narrow hem at the top edge, then fold the bag and stitch across the bottom and up one side. I like to tie the top with a fancy ribbon. In the photo the orange bag holds a cardboard tube: it is tied with a strip of silk with a gold edge. The mauve bag is tied with a piece of green pleated fabric left over from the Pleated Vest project on page 54. A rose decorates this bag. The multicolored bag in the center was a special piece of overpainted fabric.

Ribbons

Ribbons or fasteners can be of any style and material. I used a piece of purple pleated fabric to wrap around one gift; for others, I made roses out of folded painted fabric. I even painted a commercial silk rose and cut off the stem, to decorate one small bag. Other ribbons are painted wire-edged ribbons or tubes made by sewing long strips of painted silk together.

The fun of making your own wrappings is to experiment and be inventive. Sometimes I have to fasten the top of a bag with a twist tie because I made the bag too small. I just cover the tie with a ribbon or piece of fabric. Other times I fasten the bag with a rubber band. I have even used a safety pin to secure my fancy gift wrapping. Friends and family who receive my gifts know that sewing and creativity are my life, so a pin or twist tie on a gift only makes it more special.

I hope you enjoy trying the projects in this book. I had a wonderful time designing them. Someday we will meet, and you can share your projects with me.

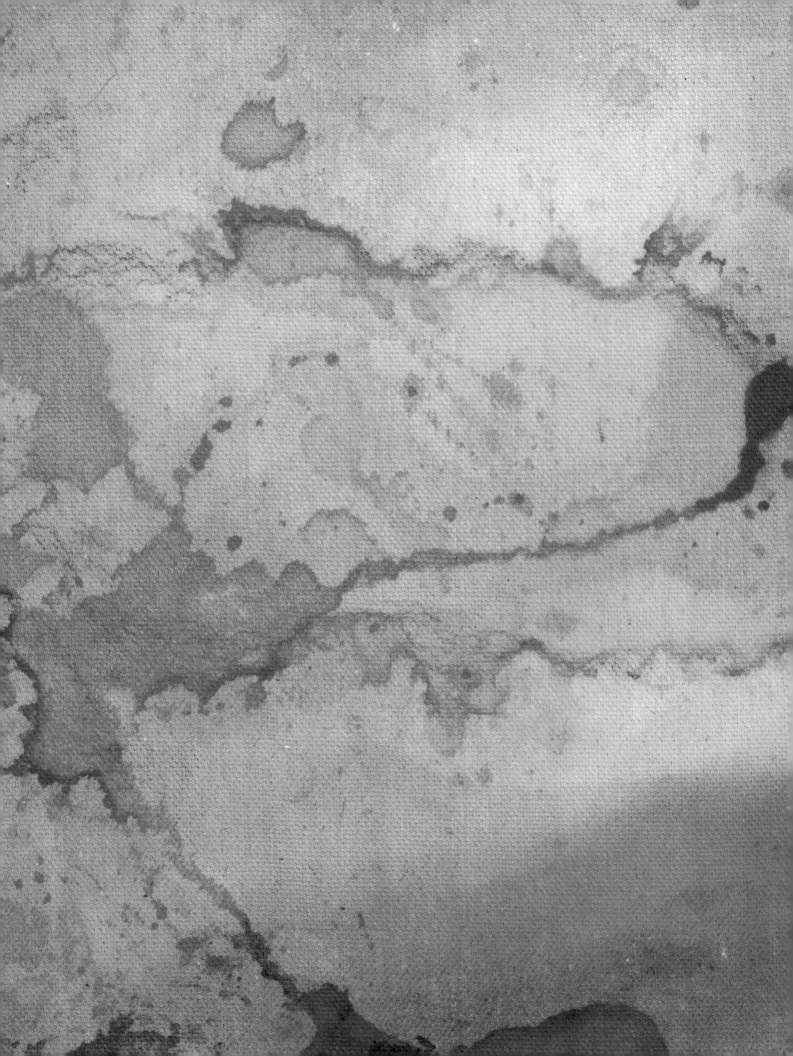

About the Author

Yvonne Porcella is a native Californian whose family grew produce in the coastal valleys. One of her early memories of going to the packing shed includes the ritual of applying the colorful labels to the harvest boxes. She learned to sew clothing from her mother, and the whole family made Christmas cards and other artistic projects together. We see these early influences shaping her present career and this book. However, by the age of five she had determined to become a nurse. She was a member of the inaugural class at the University of San Francisco School of Nursing and worked as an operating-room nurse while raising four children. In 1979 she returned to the early influences, deciding to spend her life as an artist.

The earliest part of her new career was spent as a hand weaver. She originated a contemporary tapestry technique, designed a project for a national magazine, and mounted a one-woman gallery exhibition of wearable art and weavings in 1972. During the 1970's, her work appeared in many books, including the landmark *Creating Body Coverings* by Joyce Aiken and Jean Ray Laury. She began to teach weaving and wearable art classes throughout the country.

She is also well known today as a studio art quilt artist. Her work was included in six Quilt National shows and in the exhibition The Art Quilt, organized by Michael Kile and Penny McMorris, which toured under the auspices of the Smithsonian Institution. Her work is in the permanent collections of the High Museum in Atlanta, the American Craft Museum in New York, the Los Angeles County Museum of Art, the Oakland Museum, and the Phoenix Art Museum. Much of her work appears in major quilt shows, decorative art galleries, museum exhibitions, and private and corporate collections. She has lectured and taught widely on four continents, on a diverse range of topics, and she hosted the Yvonne Porcella Quilt Symposium in Modesto, California. She is the founder and President of the Board of Directors of Studio Art Quilt Associates, a national non-profit corporation dedicated to the promotion of art quilts. Her work has appeared in many books and magazines internationally, and three of her earlier books *(Pieced Clothing, Pieced Clothing Variations, Yvonne Porcella: A Colorful Book)* are still in print and available from C&T Publishing.

Yvonne is known especially for her strengths in art clothing and quilting, and for her individualistic combinations of colors. She is an artist who handles color vibrantly and with an apparently endless palette. Her work is bold, using pure color in dynamic relationships. She also hand paints fabrics to achieve a soft, pastel, watercolor effect and uses a variety of these fabrics to create pleasing compositions—as in this book.

She and her husband continue to live in California, dividing their time between homes in the central valley and the Sierra Foothills.

For information on workshops and lectures:
Yvonne Porcella Studios
3619 Shoemake Avenue
Modesto, CA 95358

Resource Guide

Fabric Paint

Binney & Smith Inc.
P. O. Box 431
Easton, PA 18042
Liquitex, Interference, gesso

Cerulean Blue Ltd.
P. O. Box 21168
Seattle, WA 98111-3168
(206) 323-8600
Cloud Cover, Lumière

Color Craft Ltd.
14 Airport Park Rd
East Granby, CT 06026
(203) 653-5505
Textile Colors by Createx

Craft Industries Limited
P. O. Box 38
Somerset, MA 02726-0038
(508) 676-3883
Setacolor

Decart, Inc.
Morrisville, VT 05661
(802) 888-4217
Deka Permanent Fabric Paints

Dharma Trading Co.
P. O. Box 150916
San Rafael, CA 94915
(800) 542-5227
(415) 456-7657
Setacolor, brushes, fabric pens & markers, Jacquard Textile Colors, Versatex Printing Paint

Pebeo France
Siège Social—Usine
St-Marcel
13367 Marseille Cedex 11
France
Tel. 91 35 90 40
Setacolor

Pebeo
1035 St-Denis
Sherbrooke, PQ
Canada J1K 2S7
Setacolor (wholesale)

Setacolor is available retail in Canada from
Maiwa Hand Prints
(604) 669-3939

Rupert, Gibbon & Spider, Inc.
P. O. Box 425
Healdsburg, CA 95448
(800) 442-0455
Jacquard

Siphon Art
P. O. Box 150710
San Rafael, CA 94915-0710
(510) 236-0949
Versatex

Daler-Rowney U.S.A.
4 Corporate Drive
Cranbury, NJ 08512
(609) 655-5252
Pearlescent Liquid Acrylic

Daler-Rowney
9 Peacock Lane
Bracknell, Berkshire RG12 4ST
England
Tel. 0 344 424 621
Pearlescent Liquid Acrylic

Tulip Paint
24 Prime Park Way
Natick, MA 01760
Tulip paint

Batting

Fairfield Processing Corporation
P.O. Box 1130
Danbury, CT 06813
(800) 980-8000
Cotton Classic, Low Loft, Poly-fil

Hobbs Bonded Fibers
P.O. Box 3000
Mexia, TX 76667
(800) 433-3357
Thermore

Cotton and Silk Fabrics

Dharma Trading Co.
P. O. Box 150916
San Rafael, CA 94915
(800) 542-5227
(415) 456-7657
Silk and cotton fabrics, scarves, accessories, fabric pens and markers

Exotic Silks (wholesale)
1959 Leghorn
Mtn. View, CA 94043
(800) 845-SILK
(415) 965-0712
Silk fabrics, scarves, clothing

Rupert, Gibbon & Spider, Inc.
P.O. Box 425
Healdsburg, CA 95448
(800) 442-0455
Silk and cotton fabrics, scarves, silk clothing and ties

Sureway Trading Enterprises
826 Pine Ave., Suite 5-6
Niagara Falls, NY 14301
(416) 596-1887
Silk fabrics, scarves

Testfabrics, Inc.
P. O. Box 420
Middlesex, NJ 08846
(201) 469-6446
Silk and cotton fabrics, silk scarves

Qualin International
P. O. Box 31145
San Francisco, CA 94131
(415) 647-1329
Silk fabrics, scarves, clothing

Thai Silks (retail)
252 State St.
Los Altos, CA 94022
(800) 722-SILK
(415) 948-3426
Silk fabrics

UTEX Trading
710 - 9th St. Suite 5
Niagara Falls, NY 14301
(416) 596-7565 ext. 38
Silk fabrics

Silk Ribbon and Exclusive Silk Ribbon Roses

Elsie's Exquisiques
208 State St.
St. Joseph, MI 49085
(800) 742-SILK
(616) 982-0449
Silk ribbons, silk ribbon roses

Silk Ribbon

Judith Designs
P. O. Box 177
Castle Rock, CO 80104
Silk ribbon

Hand-Painted and Hand-Dyed Fabrics

Shades Inc.
Stacy Michell
585 Cobb Parkway S.
Nunn Complex Studio O
Marietta, GA 30062
(404) 919-9824
Hand-dyed cotton fabrics

Sky Dyes
Micky Lawler
83 Richmond Lane
West Hartford, CT 06117
(203) 232-1429
Hand-painted silk fabrics

Sonya Lee Barrington
Dying to Quilt
837 - 47th Ave.
San Francisco, CA 94121
(415) 221-6510
Hand-dyed cotton fabrics and marbled fabrics

Lunn Fabrics Inc.
Debra Lunn and Michael Mrowka
357 Santa Fe Drive
Denver, CO 80223
Hand-dyed, airbrushed, silk screened, and hand-stamped cotton fabrics

Tools

Excel Hobby Blade Corp.
481 Getty Ave.
Paterson, NJ 07503
(800) 433-6538
(201) 278-4000
Hemostats, rotary cutters and mats

General Pencil Company
P. O. Box 5311
3160 Bay Rd.
Redwood City, CA 94063
(415) 369-7169
"The Master's' Brush Cleaner

General Pencil Company
67 Fleet St.
Jersey City, NJ 07306
(201) 653-2298
"The Master's" Brush Cleaner

Omnigrid Inc.
1560 Port Drive
Burlington, WA 98233
(800) 755-3530
Omnigrid rulers

Metallic Pens

FaberCastell Corporation
551 Spring Place Road
Lewisburg, TN 37091
(800) 835-8382
Uni pens

Pilot Corporation of America
Turnbull, CT 06611
Pilot pens

Uchida of America Corporation
New York/California
Deco Color, Liquid Gold (can be used in place of Uni and Pilot)

Glue Sticks

FaberCastell Corporation
551 Spring Place Road
Lewisburg, TN 37091
(800) 835-8382
UHU stic glue sticks

Metallic Thread

Kreinik Mfg. Co., Inc.
9199 Reisterstown Rd.
Suite 209B
Owings Mills, MD 21117
(800) 537-2166
(410) 581-5088
Cord and Ombré metallic threads

Other Fine Quilting Books From C&T Publishing

An Amish Adventure, Roberta Horton
Appliqué 12 Easy Ways! Elly Sienkiewicz
Appliqué 12 Borders and Medallions! Elly Sienkiewicz
The Art of Silk Ribbon Embroidery, Judith Montano
*Baltimore Album Quilts, Historic Notes and Antique
  Patterns*, Elly Sienkiewicz
*Baltimore Album Revival! Historic Quilts in the Making.
  The Catalog of C&T Publishing's Quilt Show and
  Contest*, Elly Sienkiewicz
Baltimore Beauties and Beyond (2 Volumes), Elly
  Sienkiewicz
*The Best From Gooseberry Hill: Patterns For Stuffed
  Animals & Dolls*, Kathy Pace
Boston Commons Quilt, Blanche Young and Helen
  Young Frost
Calico and Beyond, Roberta Horton
A Celebration of Hearts, Jean Wells and Marina
  Anderson
Christmas Traditions From the Heart, Margaret Peters
Christmas Traditions From the Heart, Volume Two,
  Margaret Peters
A Colorful Book, Yvonne Porcella
Colors Changing Hue, Yvonne Porcella
Crazy Quilt Handbook, Judith Montano
Crazy Quilt Odyssey, Judith Montano
Design a Baltimore Album Quilt! Elly Sienkiewicz
Dimensional Appliqué—Baskets, Blooms & Borders, Elly
  Sienkiewicz
Elegant Stitches, Judith Baker Montano
*Fantastic Figures: Ideas & Techniques Using the New
  Clays*, Susanna Oroyan
Flying Geese Quilt, Blanche Young and Helen Young
  Frost
14,287 Pieces of Fabrics and Other Poems, Jean Ray Laury
Friendship's Offering, Susan McKelvey
Happy Trails, Pepper Cory
Heirloom Machine Quilting, Harriet Hargrave
Imagery on Fabric, Jean Ray Laury
Irish Chain Quilt, Blanche Young and Helen Young
  Frost
Isometric Perspective, Katie Pasquini-Masopust
Landscapes & Illusions, Joen Wolfrom
Let's Make Waves, Marianne Fons and Liz Porter
The Magical Effects of Color, Joen Wolfrom
Mariner's Compass, Judy Mathieson
Mastering Machine Appliqué, Harriet Hargrave
Memorabilia Quilting, Jean Wells
The New Lone Star Handbook, Blanche Young and Helen
  Young Frost

NSA Series: Bloomin' Creations, Jean Wells
NSA Series: Holiday Magic, Jean Wells
NSA Series: Hometown, Jean Wells
NSA Series: Fans, Hearts, & Folk Art, Jean Wells
Pattern Play, Doreen Speckmann
Perfect Pineapples, Jane Hall and Dixie Haywood
Picture This, Jean Wells and Marina Anderson
Pieced Clothing, Yvonne Porcella
Pieced Clothing Variations, Yvonne Porcella
Plaids and Stripes, Roberta Horton
PQME Series: Basket Quilt, Jean Wells
PQME Series: Bear's Paw Quilt, Jean Wells
PQME Series: Country Bunny Quilt, Jean Wells
PQME Series: Milky Way Quilt, Jean Wells
PQME Series: Nine-Patch Quilt, Jean Wells
PQME Series: Pinwheel Quilt, Jean Wells
PQME Series: Sawtooth Star Quilt, Jean Wells
PQME Series: Stars & Hearts Quilt, Jean Wells
Patchwork Quilts Made Easy, Jean Wells (co-published
  with Rodale)
Quilts for Fabric Lovers, Alex Anderson
Quilts, Quilts, and More Quilts! Diana McClun and
  Laura Nownes
Recollections, Judith Montano
Stitching Free: Easy Machine Pictures, Shirley Nilsson
Story Quilts, Mary Mashuta
Symmetry: A Design System for Quiltmakers, Ruth B.
  McDowell
3 Dimensional Design, Katie Pasquini
A Treasury of Quilt Labels, Susan McKelvey
Trip Around the World Quilts, Blanche Young and Helen
  Young Frost
Virginia Avery's Hats, A Heady Affair
Virginia Avery's Nifty Neckwear
Visions: The Art of the Quilt, Quilt San Diego
Visions: Quilts, Layers of Excellence, Quilt San Diego
Whimsical Animals, Miriam Gourley
Wearable Art for Real People, Mary Mashuta

For more information write for a free catalog from
C&T Publishing
P.O. Box 1456
Lafayette, CA 94549
(1-800-284-1114)